AGAINST ALL ODDS
my story

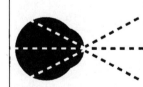

This Large Print Book carries the
Seal of Approval of N.A.V.H.

AGAINST ALL ODDS

my story

CHUCK NORRIS

with Ken Abraham

Thorndike Press • Waterville, Maine

Published in 2005 by arrangement with Broadman & Holman Publishers.

Thorndike Press® Large Print Biography.

The tree indicium is a trademark of Thorndike Press.

The text of this Large Print edition is unabridged.
Other aspects of the book may vary from the original edition.

Set in 16 pt. Plantin by Ramona Watson.

Printed in the United States on permanent paper.

Library of Congress Cataloging-in-Publication Data

Norris, Chuck.
    Against all odds : my story / by Chuck Norris with Ken Abraham.
      p. cm.
    ISBN 0-7862-7519-7 (lg. print : hc : alk. paper)
    1. Norris, Chuck, 1940–   2. Martial artists — United States — Biography. 3. Actors — United States — Biography. I. Abraham, Ken. II. Title.
GV1113.N67A29 2004
    796.8′092—dc22
                                           2004031004

Dedication

To Rachel Joy Scott

A courageous victim of the Columbine High School shooting in Littleton, Colorado. Facing death itself, Rachel refused to compromise her faith in God. This poem, written by her father, Darrell Scott, aptly describes the problems we face, and provides the answer, for those courageous enough to believe:

Your laws ignore our deepest needs,
Your words are empty air.
You've stripped our heritage,
You've outlawed simple prayer.
Now gunshots fill our classrooms,
And precious children die.
You seek for answers everywhere,
And ask the question, "Why?"
You regulate restrictive laws,
Through legislative creed,
And yet you fail to understand
That God is what we need!

I also dedicate this book to the two most influential women in my life — my mom, Wilma Knight, and my wife, Gena.

It is impossible to overestimate the tremendous impact Mom has had on me, modeling an unconditional love, coupled with tremendous faith in God. Thank you, Mom, for your spiritual guidance, for teaching me to look for the good in every person, and for living your life with such a positive attitude — despite the circumstances, against all odds.

And to Gena, my loving wife, my soul mate, the woman who helped me see afresh what really matters in life. This book would not exist had it not been for your faith, nor would our precious babies, and I know I would not be where I am with God without your love and encouragement.

Thank you! I love you!

As the Founder/CEO of NAVH, the only national health agency solely devoted to those who, although not totally blind, have an eye disease which could lead to serious visual impairment, I am pleased to recognize Thorndike Press★ as one of the leading publishers in the large print field.

Founded in 1954 in San Francisco to prepare large print textbooks for partially seeing children, NAVH became the pioneer and standard setting agency in the preparation of large type.

Today, those publishers who meet our standards carry the prestigious "Seal of Approval" indicating high quality large print. We are delighted that Thorndike Press is one of the publishers whose titles meet these standards. We are also pleased to recognize the significant contribution Thorndike Press is making in this important and growing field.

Lorraine H. Marchi, L.H.D.
Founder/CEO
NAVH

★ Thorndike Press encompasses the following imprints: Thorndike, Wheeler, Walker and Large Print Press.

Contents

Acknowledgments

Just as filming a movie or a television series requires the assistance and expertise of numerous talented and dedicated individuals working together to accomplish a common goal, writing and publishing a book is a collaborative effort among many highly skilled and deeply committed people.

I am truly grateful to my wife, Gena, for encouraging me to write this book, and to Joe Hyams, for helping us with the first draft. A providential conversation with author Tim LaHaye led me to literary agent Mark Sweeney and writer Ken Abraham, two men who envisioned this book five years before we ever met! They not only helped me fulfill the vision of this book, but we have also become dear friends.

Special thanks to Ken Stephens, David Shepherd, Len Goss, Kim Overcash, Paul Mikos, and the tremendously enthusiastic sales representatives of Broadman & Holman Publishers. Thank you all for helping me to share my story.

Thanks, too, to my wonderful office staff — Marie, Kim, Laura, Howard, Bobby and Cynthia, Margurita, and Ilona — for their tireless efforts in keeping everything going, making my life easier, and allowing me the time to work on this book.

Thanks to the administrative staff and instructors of **KICK**START for their hard work and dedication. They are impacting thousands of young lives across America.

Thanks to our family members and friends, and to the many people who have touched my life, encouraging me to use my God-given talents in positive ways.

Most of all, I thank God for being the driving force in my life!

All of Mr. Norris's profits from this book will be donated to **KICK**START, the organization he founded to help young people develop self-esteem and positive values through the martial arts. For more information, contact:

Chuck Norris
Top Kick Productions
18653 Ventura Boulevard, Suite 751
Tarzana, CA 91356
www.chucknorris.com

CHAPTER 1

A Wake-up Call

I could tell that something was wrong the moment I caught my security guard's eye. I was in Washington, D.C., seated on the dais as a special guest of the newly elected President of the United States, George W. Bush. About five thousand of the president's friends — many of whom had played key roles in helping George W. Bush get elected — were in attendance, the men decked out in tuxedoes and the women in extravagant evening gowns. The first Presidential Dinner of the new administration had been a happy, gala affair, and I had enjoyed the evening immensely.

At about 10:30 p.m., the President and First Lady said good-night and had exited the room, and I was getting ready to follow suit. I stepped off the platform, shaking hands and greeting each person as I made my way through the crowd. The room was filled with friendly faces, so it struck me as odd when I noticed my security guard, Phil Cameron, frowning and motioning in my direction. I knew something must be seriously wrong, or Phil would never interrupt me on such a momentous occasion. I wedged my way through the well-wishers until Phil and I were standing side-by-side.

"We've had an emergency telephone call, Mr. Norris. Your wife is in the hospital; she's going into preterm labor."

"What? That can't be! Gena is only twenty-three weeks along; she is nowhere near the thirty-eight weeks of a full-term pregnancy!"

"I don't know anything about that, sir. All I know is that she told me to contact you as soon as possible."

I rushed to the phone and called the hospital. The operator connected me to Gena's room, and when she answered, I could tell that she had been crying.

"Sweetheart, I'm so sorry I'm not there with you. Are you OK?"

"I'm fine, but I needed to get to the hospital right away. They have to surgically close my cervix to save our babies."

I could tell by the quiver in her voice that Gena was trying desperately to hold her emotions in check.

"Carlos, I'm scared," she admitted as she started to cry. "I'm scared for our babies."

"Honey, I'm calling the pilots right now. I'll be by your side just as fast as the jet can get me there."

We were expecting twins, a boy and a girl. Gena and I had already seen them on the ultrasound machine in the doctor's office, watching excitedly like two young kids ourselves as our babies moved around, bumping into each other in Gena's crowded womb. We'd even named them already; our little girl we named Danilee and our little boy, Dakota.

The pregnancy had been horrendously difficult for Gena. She'd given birth twice before, so she knew the ropes when it came to being pregnant. But carrying these two "miracle babies" had been a heavy load from the beginning. At several points along the way, we'd come close to losing the twins, or Gena, or all three of them. A beautiful yet tough woman, Gena had withstood several highly unusual medical challenges that threatened to end her life, or those of our babies. Had she not been mentally and spiritually strong, and in such excellent physical condition prior to becoming pregnant, her body might not have been able to endure the strain.

When the invitation from the President's office had arrived in our mailbox several weeks earlier, Gena and I were excited about attending. But as the event drew nearer, we realized it might be dangerous for Gena and our babies to be flying across the country from California to Washington, D.C., especially in light of the complications we'd already experienced during the pregnancy. We decided it would be best for Gena to remain at home, and I'd take my brother, Aaron, along with me, and our good friends, Dennis Berman, a successful Dallas businessman who had agreed to be our children's godparent, and John Hensley, the former head of US Customs. Phil Cameron, my personal protection officer, who often accompanied me to events where I'd be in large crowds, had flown ahead to Washington a few days earlier to make sure the details of my trip were in order.

The four of us flew to Washington on a private chartered jet the day of the event. Phil joined us at the Pentagon. We were ushered out to the Pentagon Promenade, where we were greeted by the Air Police honor guard, and I received an achievement award from the Air Force for being an outstanding airman. They also made me an honorary Air Force recruiter. We posed for a photograph on the Promenade, in the exact spot where 9-11 terrorists would crash an airliner a few months later. We spent the remainder of our afternoon touring the Pentagon, having lunch with several generals, and enjoying a fascinating visit with Secret Service Director Brian L. Stafford. We planned to return to California the following morning.

Prior to the Presidential Dinner, the new President and First Lady, Laura Bush, and I posed for a special picture to commemorate the occasion. Ever gracious, the president thanked me for my support and for being a friend of the Bush family. It had been a day to remember, and I could hardly wait to call Gena after the dinner to tell her all about it. . . .

But now Gena was lying in a hospital emergency room in California. Suddenly what really matters in life came into clear focus. In a moment, with one sentence my entire priority list had been altered.

"Call the pilots, Phil. Tell them that we're leaving right now!"

"Yes, sir."

I wanted to get to Gena as soon as possible, so as soon as Phil could rouse the pilots, I wanted to be in the air.

I said my good-byes to the remaining dignitaries still at the gala while Phil contacted the pilots. Between shaking hands, smiling, and offering best wishes, I'd glance in Phil's direction, waiting for his signal that told me we were on our way. It didn't come.

Instead, the look on Phil's face told me that he wasn't pleased. "I've got the pilot on the phone," Phil said, "but you may want to talk to him." Phil handed his cell phone to me.

I took the phone and said, "What's the problem?"

The pilot spoke haltingly, "I'm sorry, Mr. Norris, but my copilot has had a beer, and I'd prefer not to fly tonight."

"What? What do you mean, you prefer not to fly?"

"Well, we really weren't planning on going back to LA tonight, so I didn't think it would matter for him to have a drink. But since he did, it's against regulations for us to fly tonight."

I was furious, but I knew the pilot was right. Under different circumstances, I might even have appreciated his integrity and truthfulness. After all, the pilot could have easily deceived me; he didn't have to tell me. I'd have never known that his copilot had taken a drink, and in light of the emergency back home, I might not have cared!

"How soon can we leave?" I asked.

"Not before five-thirty tomorrow morning," the pilot replied.

"Five-thirty!" I looked at my watch. It was only eleven o'clock.

There was nothing left to do but try to find alternative transportation. Aaron, Dennis, John, Phil, and I hurried back to my room at the Ritz Carlton Hotel. We tried desperately to get a commercial flight out but to no avail. We called every place we could find, hoping to hire another private plane in D.C., but the earliest we could get another crew to depart was at three-thirty.

Pacing back and forth in the room, my mind raced with the obvious contradictions. I felt so helpless. I had been a six-time World Karate Champion; I had starred in more than twenty-three motion pictures in which I had played a hero; I had more recently starred in *Walker, Texas Ranger*, my own television series, for eight years, again playing the hero; yet there was nothing I could do to help my wife.

I had earned millions of dollars over my

lifetime. I'd been a friend to several presidents, yet all the money in my bank account couldn't help me now. My friendships with men and women of influence were not enough.

There was only one person to whom I could turn. I prayed, "Oh, God, please take care of my wife and our babies."

Phil gave me his cell phone to call Gena at the hospital to tell her that we'd been delayed. I was able to reach her, but she was so distraught and groggy, I could hardly discern a word she said. Gena was able to communicate to me that she was going to be operated on at eight o'clock the following morning. Apparently, the doctor had presented a bleak scenario as he explained to Gena all the things that might go wrong. I told her that I'd get home as soon as I could. I tried to encourage her; we prayed briefly over the phone and said our good-byes. "I love you, Sweetheart. I'll be with you soon."

Our bags were packed and sitting right by the hotel room door, ready to go. I was too frustrated to sleep, so the guys and I stayed up all night, talking, pacing, praying, and ticking the minutes off the clock.

At five-thirty sharp we were rolling down

the runway. The moment our plane landed in California, I bounded down the steps and raced to the hospital, arriving around ten o'clock Pacific Time. Gena was already in the recovery room.

As I stepped inside the room, I saw Gena lying in bed, covered by a crisp white sheet. She looked so pale and fragile. The woman whom I had grown to depend on in all facets of my life now seemed so frail. I leaned over and kissed her gently. "Baby, I'm so sorry I wasn't here for you. . . ." I started to apologize. "I'm never going to leave you again!"

"You're here now," she said. "That's all that matters."

I looked at the woman who loved me so much that she was willing to step into the valley of the shadow of death to give birth to our children. The doctor had said that if we could keep Gena in bed for the next ten weeks or so, he felt sure that the babies would be fine. Gena's commitment to do whatever was necessary for the benefit of her children reminded me of another woman of tremendous faith, my mom. My mom had gone through awful travail trying to bring me into this world. In fact, like Gena and our babies, my mom and I had to struggle against the odds to survive.

CHAPTER 2

Mixed Motivators

My mother, Wilma Norris, was only eighteen years of age when she gave birth to me, after enduring an exhausting seven days in labor! She went to the hospital on Sunday, March 3, and I was not born until the following Sunday. Several times during the difficult delivery, the doctors feared they were going to lose her or me — or both of us. Finally, in the early hours of March 10, 1940, I weighed in at six pounds, eight ounces. But Mom's concerns were far from over. Something wasn't right. My skin color was all wrong!

My tiny body was a dark shade of bluish purple. My father, Ray Norris, was in the delivery room along with both of my grandmothers, and when he first caught a glimpse of me, he was so unnerved that he fainted right on the spot.

The doctors and nurses weren't too concerned about my dad, but they were extremely concerned about me! They recognized me as a "blue baby," which means that I had not begun breathing immediately after birth, thus causing my skin to turn the deathly color. They had to act fast to save my life, even faster to prevent the lack of oxygen from doing permanent damage to my brain. The doctors hastily placed me on oxygen to jump start my lungs. It worked, and before long, I was gulping air like a pro.

Nevertheless, for the first five days of my life, the doctors weren't sure I was going to make it. They kept me in an isolation unit, similar to a neonatal intensive care unit nowadays, to prevent me from contamination and also to keep a close watch on me. I was too weak to eat normally, so Mom expressed milk for me, and I was fed with an eyedropper. Extremely weak herself, Mom was not permitted to see me during that time. She still has a letter written by my grandmother, dated that week, telling my aunt that "Wilma's baby probably isn't going to live."

But Mom and I surprised everyone! We pulled through, and before long the doctors discharged my mother and me. Mom later told me that from the first moment she saw me, she looked into my face and said, "God has plans for you." It was a message she has reiterated many times throughout my life.

Mom and Dad took me home to the farm where Dad worked, in Ryan, Oklahoma, a small town not far from the Texas border, about a two-hour drive from Dallas. The name on my birth certificate is Carlos Ray Norris. I was named in honor of Reverend Carlos Berry, my family's minister in Ryan. My middle name, Ray, is in honor of my father.

Genetically speaking, I am equal parts Irish and Native American. On the Norris side, my paternal grandfather was Irish, and my paternal grandmother was a full-blooded Cherokee Indian. My mother's family name was Scarberry. My maternal grandmother, Agnes, was Irish, while my maternal grandfather was a Cherokee Indian from Kentucky.

Grandpa Norris left Ireland and came to America with his parents in the mid-1800s. He married and had three children, but his wife died from the hardships of frontier life. He hired a sixteen-year-old Indian girl from the Cherokee Indian reservation to be the children's nanny. Before long he decided to marry the nanny, and arranged to buy her from her parents on the reservation. The fact that the young woman was in love with a young man from her own tribe was of no significance to her parents. They sold her to my grandfather without a moment's hesitation.

The young Cherokee woman proved to be a good choice. She bore Grandpa Norris thirteen children, seven of whom lived, including my dad. Nevertheless, their relationship never blossomed into romantic love — perhaps my grandma could not forget her first true love from whom she had been ripped away to marry my grandpa. Years later my mom told me that at Grandpa Norris's funeral, Grandma said, "Good. Now I'm finally rid of him!" Not exactly the mourning of a grief-stricken widow!

My parents were a handsome couple. Dad was about six feet, one inch, well built and strong, with coal black hair and black eyes. In early photos he resembles John Wayne as a young man. Dad was nineteen and Mom sixteen when they married in Marietta, Oklahoma. Mom was a petite young woman, with long, flowing red hair and a pretty face full of freckles.

We soon moved from Ryan to Lawton, Oklahoma, where Dad got a job as a mechanic with the Greyhound Bus Company. It was the first of at least a dozen moves our family made before I reached the age of twelve. Had it not been for Mom's spiritual and practical stability, we'd have established no roots at all. Her love was the glue that kept us together and provided us with a sense of security, no matter where we moved or how often we packed up and moved again.

In November 1942, Dad took Mom and me to Wilson, Oklahoma, to stay with Granny Scarberry while he went to Richmond, California, hoping to get a job in the shipyards. The war was raging, and Dad felt that if he could contribute to the effort by working in the shipyard, he could serve his country and still avoid being drafted and leaving his young family. He was wrong, but his ploy provided him a few extra months to find a place for us to live.

Mom was five months pregnant at the time. We stayed with Granny another month and then took a train to California to be with Dad. Traveling on the same train was a group of young Navy sailors who took me under their wing. They recognized that Mom was pregnant, so they helped take care of me. It took several days to make the trip from Oklahoma to California, so when the train stopped in small towns along the way, the sailors disembarked long enough to run into the station or into town to get Mom and me something to eat. They were good guys, and I was in awe of them. My respect for the US military had its beginnings right there on that train.

Two months later my brother, Wieland, was born. Mom planned to name him Jimmy, but Dad named him Wieland — after his favorite beer. Mom was upset, but there was nothing she could do. The name was already on the birth certificate.

Three months later Dad was drafted into the army and was soon fighting the Nazis in Germany. While Dad was away in the service, Mom, Wieland, and I moved back to live with Granny Scarberry in her tiny home in Wilson, Oklahoma. Wilson was a small prairie town, flat, arid, and dusty, with a population of about one thousand people. It was an impoverished and desolate area, just a few miles east of the Texas-Oklahoma border. That's where I spent most of my early, formative years.

Granny Scarberry's home was a small clapboard house on the outskirts of Wilson. All four of us — Mom, Granny, Wieland, and I — slept in one room.

Granny slept in the bed, while Mom, Wieland, and I took the couch that folded out into a bed. My brother and I were bathed together in a big galvanized tin washtub. Our toilet was an outhouse, and it reeked so horribly, I hated going in there! Many times I'd walk to my aunt's home over a mile away to use the bathroom because she had indoor plumbing. It was worth the walk!

Although Granny Scarberry possessed little as far as material goods, she was a saint. A tiny woman with bright blue dancing eyes, Granny's heart overflowed with a love for God and for her family. She showered Wieland and me with attention and affection. Granny's love filled that shack in which we lived and made it a home.

Dad had been overseas for more than two years when a young boy, riding a bicycle, came to our house delivering a telegram from the War Department. Mom signed for the telegram and, with her hands shaking, hurried to open it. Suddenly she began screaming! Granny raced across the room and pulled Mom close to her. "What's wrong, Wilma? What's wrong?"

"Ray is missing in action," I heard Mom

sob, holding the telegram out for Granny to see. I was too young to know what "missing in action" meant, but by the way Mom and Granny were acting, it sounded as though Dad might not be coming home for a long time or maybe not at all.

I was concerned for my dad, but I wasn't worried about our family surviving. As long as my mother and Granny Scarberry were around, I felt safe. Every night before we went to bed, we all knelt together in our living room and prayed, asking God to find my dad and to send him home to us.

For three long months we heard nothing at all. Then at last we received good news. Dad was alive! He had been shot in the leg and nearly buried alive in a German foxhole, causing him to be separated from his unit. When the debris was cleared, his comrades found him. He was transferred home to Texas and was recovering in a military hospital. The doctors estimated that within two months Dad would be returning home to us.

For the next two months I'd sit out on the porch every day, waiting for the bus to pull up. Each day I'd watch as men and women got off the bus, my eyes peeled for any sign of Dad. Disappointed, I'd go back inside and say, "Not today, Mom. Dad didn't come home."

After two months passed, I was becoming discouraged. One day I watched and waited for the bus to unload its passengers, only to be disappointed again. I started back inside the house and said, "Mom, I don't think Dad is ever coming home."

"Oh, really?" Mom said just then with a twinkle in her eye. "Well, guess who that is!" She pointed to a soldier slowly easing himself off the bus. It was Dad!

The good news was that Dad was back in the USA. The bad news was that his drinking problem, already serious before he'd gone off to war, was now even worse.

CHAPTER 3

Life in a Bottle

Growing up, my most difficult and confusing relationship was with my father. One of the few positive memories I have of him is the day he picked me up and let me straddle his broad shoulders while he carried me to the banks of the Red River, looking across the water toward Texas. We spent the entire day fishing and talking, just the two of us. When I flash back on that scene now, it seems like an image I saw in a movie: father and son on a riverbank with fishing lines stabbed out over shining water — a perfect image of togetherness. But as soon as we got home with the few fish we had caught, Dad left for the local beer joint. He didn't return until much later that night, drunk again.

One night, Dad and my Uncle Buck wanted to go out drinking and they needed some money. Mom had only five dollars left with which to buy food for Wieland

and me, and she refused to give it to Dad. "Just take that money from Wilma," Uncle Buck urged.

"That's right. Give me that money!" Dad bellowed.

"No, Ray," Mom replied calmly. "You're not going to get this money. I'm saving it to buy food for the children."

Uncle Buck cajoled my dad, "Ray, punch her in the mouth and get that money." Buck punched his hand with his fist, menacingly. Dad formed a fist and shook it in Mom's face.

Standing tall at five foot, two inches, Mom didn't flinch. She looked my dad right in the eyes and said, "You go ahead and hit me, but you're going to have to sleep sometime. And when you do, I'm going to get a frying pan and beat you to death!"

Dad unclenched his fist, and he and Buck stormed out of the house — without Mom's five dollars.

Dad was generally a good man when he was sober, but those sober days were becoming fewer and further between. When he was drunk, little things often sent him into a rage. If he heard the water running while he was suffering from a hangover, he would explode in an abusive tirade, roaring threats and expletives against everyone in the house. While Mom tried to calm him down, Wieland and I hid in the bedroom.

Despite Dad's bombast Mom was the disciplinarian in our family. When Wieland and I got into fights, Mom would make us sit down in chairs, across from each other. We'd be huffing and puffing, our cheeks red, our necks wet with perspiration, and Mom would say, "Now sit there and look at each other, and don't say a word until I tell you to move." Wieland and I would sit there and glare at each other. Before long one of us would start to giggle, and then we'd bust up laughing. In a matter of minutes, we couldn't even remember what we had been fighting about.

When I seriously misbehaved, Mom would send me out to get a switch to swat me. Dad would say, "If you're going to spank him, I'm leaving." Dad's threats didn't deter Mom from disciplining me one bit. I received a good thrashing with the switch, and Dad went off on another drinking binge. I now realize that Dad could never stand confrontation. It was easier for him simply to run away. Sadly, he spent most of his life running.

When I was six years old, we moved to Napa, California, where we had family.

Dad went to work at a Navy shipyard, and I started school. In school I was shy and inhibited. If the teacher asked me to recite something aloud in front of the class, I would just shake my head no. I would rather get a poor grade than embarrass myself in front of the class. People who know me today from television and movies may have a hard time imagining me as shy, but believe me, as a boy, I was as bashful as could be!

Wieland was the outgoing Norris brother. But Wieland had such bad asthma that we were forced to move again, this time to Miami, Arizona, near Mom's sisters and their families. The climate was drier in Arizona, and Mom hoped that Wieland could breathe more easily there. We lived in a small cottage next to a gas station, and Mom enrolled me in the third grade. Most of the students were Native Americans. I was the new kid there and the only one with blond hair and blue eyes.

An Indian boy named Bobby was the class bully, and for some reason he had it in for me. He chased me home from school every day. He was my age but a lot larger, so I did the smart thing — I ran!

One day Bobby broke a desk during recess. The teacher accused me of being the culprit. In those days corporal punishment was common in public schools, and teachers paddled students regularly. My teacher threatened that she was going to swat me if I didn't fess up to breaking the desk. I knew that Bobby had done it, but I was not about to tell. I stood up and dutifully followed her into the hallway to endure my swats, when one of the other kids spoke up and said, "Teacher, Carlos didn't break the desk; Bobby did!" The teacher took one look at Bobby's face and quickly figured out who deserved the punishment for the broken desk. I was off the hook with her but was even more odious to Bobby. He still chased me home after school every day.

Jack, the man who owned the gas station and our cottage, got tired of watching me being chased. One day, when Jack saw Bobby chasing me again, he stopped us and said, "Son, it's time that you fought this boy."

"He's too big," I said.

"It doesn't matter," Jack said. "You can't run from your fears forever. It's time to stand up for yourself."

While Jack was talking to me, Bobby was standing nearby, ready to resume the chase. I looked over at him and then back at Jack. I knew Jack was right. I turned around and faced Bobby. I grabbed him and wrestled him to the ground. We grappled with each other and rolled back and forth in the dirt. I was getting the worst of it until I grabbed Bobby's finger and began bending it backward. Bobby burst into tears.

"Do you give up?" I shouted at him.

He nodded his head and cried, "Yes!"

I let go of his finger. And he jumped me again! I grabbed his finger once more and bent it back even farther than I had before. He started crying again and screamed, "Let go, Carlos! Let go. I give up! I really mean it this time!" I let go. Bobby never chased me again, and before long we even became friends.

Confronting Bobby the bully taught me an important lesson about fear. It can often be overcome simply by facing it.

The move to Arizona didn't help Wieland's asthma; in fact, he got worse. Mom and Dad decided that we should return to Granny's home in Wilson, but we didn't have a car and couldn't afford bus tickets for all of us. One night Dad met a man and woman in a bar and talked them into driving us to Wilson. We gathered what little clothes and possessions we had and piled into the couple's car. On the way a snowstorm stranded us in New Mexico, and we had to hole up in a small, empty room for the night. It was freezing in that room, so Mom wrapped our lone blanket around Wieland and me and pulled us close to her, trying to keep us warm.

When the storm finally cleared, we took off for Wilson again, with Wieland, Mom, and me in the back seat, and Dad and the couple in the front. Once, while Dad was driving, the other man reached back and tried to caress Mom's leg. I saw what the lecher was doing, so I reared back and kicked the man's arm as hard as I could!

"Owww!" the man cried out.

"What's going on?" Dad yelled. Mom told him what the guy had tried to do and that Carlos kicked him. Dad glared over at the owner of the car and growled, "You better stop it and keep your hands where they belong if you know what's good for you." It was a tense ride the remainder of the trip, but we eventually made it to Wilson.

Although we were happy to arrive safely at Granny's, we stayed there for only a couple of months before we were off again. Dad had managed to get a car, so we moved to Cyril, Oklahoma, where he had found a job as a truck driver. We lived in a small boarding room above a restaurant where Mom worked as a waitress.

About eight months after we settled in Cyril, Dad came home drunk late one night and announced, "Get packed. We're leaving." Mom didn't know how to drive, and she begged Dad to wait until morning, but he insisted on driving to Wilson that night. Mom made a bed for Wieland and me on top of the clothes stacked in the back seat of the car. In his inebriated condition, Dad weaved all over the road as he tried to drive. Mom was crying hysterically, begging him to stop before he killed us all or someone else.

"Keep quiet, woman!" my dad roared, "or I'll leave all of you right here in the desert!" Mom pleaded with him to take us back to Granny Scarberry's, which he finally did.

That was the regular tenor of our lives — Dad coming home drunk, acting verbally abusive and belligerent, and Mom pleading for him to stop. The tirade would continue until Dad passed out. When Dad sobered up, he would tell Mom he was sorry and would try to do better. But he never did.

Dad left again soon after that, this time

for Hawthorne, California, where he had gotten another job working for Bethlehem Steel. He said he would send for us later. In the meantime to support us, Mom found a menial job in Wilson, working in a laundry.

She never gave up praying for Dad, and she never tired of telling Wieland and me that we could make something better of our lives, that God had good things in store for us.

At the time that was tough to believe.

CHAPTER 4

A Mother's Love

I scoured the streets and highways of Wilson every day after school, searching for pop bottles on the side of the road that I returned to the grocery store. The grocer paid me two cents a bottle for regular-sized bottles and a nickel each for thirty-two-ounce bottles. I also picked up scrap iron that I sold for a penny a pound. I gave all the money I earned to Mom to help put food on the table.

One thing I looked forward to more than anything was to go to the movie theater in Wilson. When Mom could afford to give me a dime, I spent all Saturday afternoon watching the double feature and the serials, the documentaries and cartoons that ran prior to the main movies. I loved those Saturdays when I escaped into another world. The Westerns, starring men like John Wayne, Gene Autry, and Roy Rogers, provided me with positive examples of proper and moral behavior. Truth is, apart from my mother and Granny, my only role models were the cowboy heroes I saw on the screen.

Each time I walked out of the theater, I felt encouraged by the belief that there were such men. I determined that I would grow up one day to be like them. Those cowboy heroes offered a lot to a young boy longing for a male role model to emulate. Their behavior in their films was governed by the "Code of the West" — loyalty, friendship, and integrity. They were unselfish and did what was right even when the risk was great. Years later I would recall those Western heroes when I developed the kind of character I wanted to play as an actor. As a boy, however, I was only a spectator involved in a vicarious adventure.

My father was a negative role model, the kind of person I didn't want to be, a bad example to be avoided. My mother, on the other hand, had such a loving and caring nature that she more than made up for his shortcomings. She never let herself get down or depressed. Even though we had a hard life, Mom maintained a strong faith in God. She instilled that faith in her sons and kept us in church.

I still remember Mom coming home exhausted from her job at the laundry and saying that we were blessed. "As bad as things seem to be," she'd say, "many people are far worse off than we are." Mom was the most positive influence in my life, and she taught Wieland and me always to look for the good in people and in circumstances, never to dwell on the bad. She believed in determination and patience: the determination to succeed in whatever you choose to do in your life and the patience to stick with it until the goal is reached. Her belief system shaped my character and became an integral part of my life. Mom's faith became my own, and although I didn't know it at the time, I now realize that my faith in God provided the core of my inner strength.

We were so poor, I didn't have real toys to play with, so I used clothespins and an active imagination. The clothespins served as toy soldiers or cowboys. In my stash I had large pins and small ones. I made the big ones the bad guys and the little ones the good guys. When I played in the dirt in our front yard, I would set up my cast of characters and prepare for battle. I hid the big pins behind a rock or tree stump and then had the little pins jump in. I visualized the fight in my mind and decided what each pin was going to do once the battle ensued. Before the fight even started, the victory had already been won in my mind! Many years later, when I became a karate competitor, I used the same technique of visualization before each bout.

When I was ten, Mom piled Wieland and me and our meager belongings on a train to Hawthorne, California, where we joined Dad. The four of us moved into an old, rickety, twenty-foot-long aluminum trailer shaped like a teardrop. Wieland and I shared the same bed, and at night, before we said our prayers and Mom tucked us in, Mom, Wieland, and I had a ritual of singing together. One of our favorite bedtime songs was "Dear Hearts and Gentle People."

Dad quit his job and hung out at a country-western bar, not far from our trailer. Sometimes he took Wieland and me with him to the bar when Mom was working. We amused ourselves as best we could while he sat and drank with his buddies.

I always wore cowboy boots and a hat. I was a cowboy at heart even then, as I am to this day. One night Dad took Wieland and me to the bar, and after a few too many drinks, he called out to the band leader, "Hey, my boy here can sing. He sings 'Dear Hearts and Gentle People.' "

"Let's hear him," the band leader said.

Dad hoisted me onto the stage. The band struck up the music, and I sang along. Ironically, I was not scared. Looking back, I'm amazed that I had the courage to stand up on stage and sing that night, yet I couldn't muster the courage to speak in class. I guess I was similar to Mel Tillis, a country music star and actor who stuttered when he spoke but never when he sang.

I have no idea how good or bad I was, but I do remember looking for Wieland after my performance. I found him hiding under the shuffleboard table. Apparently he didn't want to be associated with my singing!

Not surprisingly we soon moved again, this time to Gardena, California, where we lived in a small, run-down old house, set on an acre of parched land, a barren peninsula surrounded by plush, beautiful homes with lush, well-manicured lawns. Ours was the only dump; all the other homes around us looked like mansions. It was embarrassing.

Our nearest neighbor was a Japanese family, Yosh and Toni Hamma and Yosh's grandmother, all of whom were wonderful people. The Hammas realized how poor we were and how we struggled constantly to have enough to eat. Often, after Toni finished grocery shopping, she came by our house and told Mom that she had bought too many groceries by mistake. "Here, Wilma, would you take the excess?" She almost made it sound as though Mom was doing her a favor by taking her food.

One day Toni came to the house with two dresses, one brown and one blue. She told Mom she could not make up her mind which one she wanted. "If you were buying a dress, which one would you choose?" she asked.

"The blue one is beautiful," Mom said.

Toni handed Mom the dress and said, "Here, this dress is for you."

Mom, Wieland, and I attended Calvary Baptist Church, down the street from our house. I was extremely involved in church activities, and I trusted Jesus Christ as my Savior and was baptized there at the age of twelve.

For Christmas that year, I saved my money that I'd earned by working in a laundry after school, and I bought my mom a special present — a picture of Jesus. We moved many more times throughout our lives, and little by little most of our possessions were destroyed or given away, but that picture of Jesus went with Mom wherever we went. She still has it hanging above her bed today. Over the years I've given my mom many presents related to our faith, some of great monetary value and others of great sentimental value or other significance. But of all the gifts I've ever given her, Mom still treasures that picture of Jesus the most.

Mom earned fifteen dollars a week, so she pledged to tithe $1.50 every week to the church. Reverend Kuester, our pastor, came to visit us occasionally, and he knew how Mom was struggling to make ends meet.

One day Pastor Kuester and his wife, Margaret, came for a visit and a time of prayer. As they were preparing to leave, Pastor Kuester handed my mother the pledge letter she had signed. "Sister Norris, the Lord knows your heart," the preacher said. "He doesn't need your money. Your love and devotion to the Lord and your sons are all that God wants from you." Mom thanked the pastor for his kindness and compassion, but she continued to give 10 percent of her income to the church, and God always provided for us, in spite of Dad.

In March 1951, Mom became pregnant, and Dad took off again. "You'll see," Mom told Wieland and me. "Things will be better when he comes back." Although I was only eleven years old, I knew better. Nothing would change in our home as long as Dad continued to drink — and he showed no signs of wanting to stop. He would come home drunk, wake us up in the middle of the night, and make us walk to the liquor store to buy a bottle of Thunderbird wine for him.

I guess you could call Dad a drifter because he certainly drifted in and out of our lives. Drifter is describing him kindly; an alcoholic gypsy would be more accurate. The attic in our house became Dad's trash can. One day I looked up in the attic, and I never forgot the sight. Literally hundreds of empty wine bottles were strewn across the attic floor. Each bottle symbolized another part of our lives that my father had thrown away.

One night when Dad came home drunk, I lay in bed and prayed to God to change Dad and have him stop drinking or help us get out of this awful situation. Mom was not able to work because she was pregnant, so we had to go on public assistance — welfare — to survive. Our only other income came from Dad's thirty-two-dollar-a-month government disability check, barely enough to cover the rent.

Mom accepted things as they were and was determined to make the best of the situation. Neither Wieland nor I had a lot of clothes or toys, but Mom always made sure we had enough to eat.

My brother Aaron was born in November 1951. When he was only ten months old, Mom went back to work to support our family. She got a job at Northrop Aircraft as a silkscreen printer, where she worked the three-to-midnight swing shift. Since we couldn't afford a babysitter, I had to rush home from school every day to babysit Wieland and Aaron, who would start crying the moment Mom left for work. The first few nights that Mom worked the late shift I could hardly wait for her to get home.

I soon discovered that if I put Aaron on my lap and rocked him in the rocking chair, he would settle down. Many times I'd rock him so long that both of us would fall asleep, and Mom would find the two of us still in the rocking chair when she got home at about twelve-thirty. I cannot count how many hours I spent in that rocking chair, holding my baby brother, but it didn't bother me. Mom had instilled in me the notion of assuming responsibility, so it seemed the natural thing to do.

One night Dad had a bad car accident and tragically killed an elderly woman. He was arrested, convicted of drunk driving and vehicular manslaughter, and sentenced to a road camp for six months. Mom took me out to see him on weekends. He looked great and seemed to be in good health. The hard work apparently agreed with him, and we prayed that when he got released, after not having a drink for six months and realizing what he had done, he would stay off liquor for good. But our hopes were quickly dashed. The moment Dad got out, he went straight to the bar.

When I turned fifteen, we moved to a slightly better house in Torrance, California, a suburb of Los Angeles. Unfortunately, Dad was becoming increasingly aggressive at home and abusive toward Mom.

One night I heard my parents arguing in their bedroom. I heard a thud, my mom screaming, and then I heard her crying. I grabbed a hammer and ran into the bedroom. "If you ever touch her again, you're going to have to deal with me!" I screamed at my dad, brandishing the hammer menacingly over his head. Luckily he was too drunk to take my threat too seriously.

The next day Mom and I talked about what we should do. We agreed that it was pointless to continue living this way with Dad, never knowing how or when he'd come home or how much more violent he might become. While Dad was away one night, Mom, Wieland, Aaron, and I packed up everything we could and moved in with my aunt and uncle. My parents divorced in 1956. I was sixteen, Wieland twelve, and Aaron four.

A year later Mom met George Knight, a foreman at Northrop, where she worked. George was not only a gentleman, he was a *gentle* man who genuinely cared for her. One night Mom said, "Carlos, I need to talk with you."

"Sure, Mom. What's up?"

"George has asked me to marry him, but before I give him an answer, I want to know how you feel about it."

I hugged my mother tightly and said, "Mom, I think George would be a fine husband and stepfather." And I truly meant it. Mom married George soon after that conversation, and after the initial awkward stage, my stepfather became one of the best things that ever happened to me.

CHAPTER 5

Life Choices

With George as part of our family, for the first time in my life, I had a caring and responsible father who gave me the opportunity to be a real teenager. One night while Mom and I were talking, I said, "Mom, I remember the first time I prayed to God to get us out of that situation with Dad. I was twelve years old and always wondered if God was listening."

Mom said, "God always listens, Carlos. Prayer opens the way for God to work, and God does hear. His answer came at the time he knew was best for us."

One afternoon when I came home from school, I found my dad in the living room of our house. I heard my mother crying in her bedroom. My father said he was there "to take care of George."

"No, you're not," I said.

"How do you plan to stop me?" he said, glaring at me.

I had been afraid of my father all of my life, but I was not going to let him hurt George, who was a gentle man and no match for him.

I motioned toward the door, and my father and I went out to the front yard and squared off to fight. I don't know whether my father saw fear or determination in my eyes, but after a long moment I saw his countenance change. "I'm not going to fight with you," he said, still with a surly voice but with more a sigh of resignation. He got into his car and drove off.

I saw him only one more time after that incident, shortly after I'd gotten out of the service in 1962. Wieland and I had driven back to Wilson to visit Granny, and we pulled up to the beer joint where we knew our dad could be found. We honked the horn, and Dad sauntered out of the bar. He walked out, waved to us, and said hello. I told him that I was married and that Dianne was expecting our first baby.

"Great," he said flatly. Then he turned on his heel and walked back into the bar. That was it. No hugs, no words of affirmation, no questions as to what Wieland and I were doing with our lives. Nothing. He simply waved and went back to his beer. Little did I know, that would be the last time I'd ever see my dad alive.

That day in the living room, however, when I faced up to my father, I learned another important lesson about fear. True courage is not the absence of fear but the control of it.

With George's encouragement, I became interested in sports. I played football and did gymnastics. I wasn't a good athlete, and I certainly didn't excel at any sport, but I enjoyed the competition. Similarly, schoolwork didn't come easily to me, but I worked hard and wound up making decent grades.

I discovered a new pride in myself, too, and began to blossom, thanks to our family unity and a strong paternal influence. Mom was able to relax a bit, now that George was part of our family. She felt that she and George were working together rather than pulling in different directions. As for me, I finally had a father figure who cared about me and was a good role model.

When I was seventeen I wanted to join the Navy with my cousin Jerry and best friend Bill, but because I was underage, I needed a parental signature to enlist. Mom wouldn't hear of it. "No, you must finish high school first," she insisted. "By then, you'll be eighteen years old and you can decide what you want to do after you graduate."

We moved from an apartment in Gardena to a house in Torrance, so I transferred from Gardena High to North Torrance High in the middle of my junior year. I was still quite shy, however, and avoided talking in front of a class. I was certain that I would say the wrong thing and my face would turn red, as it always did when I was embarrassed.

While still in my junior year, I met a girl named Dianne Holecheck, a bubbly, outgoing, brown-eyed beauty and one of the prettiest and most popular girls in school. I saw Dianne often on our school campus, but I was too shy to talk to her. Then one evening I was stocking shelves at Boys' Market, a grocery store where I worked as a box boy, and Dianne came into the store. I pretended to pay no attention, but Dianne was on a mission. She walked straight down the aisle where I was working and asked me where to find a particular grocery item. We struck up a conversation, and I was smitten with her instantly. Eventually, over the next few weeks, I worked up the courage to ask her out. From then on we were a couple. We went steady all through my last year of high school.

I continued working after school as a box boy in the market, opening boxes of canned goods and produce, stocking shelves, and hoping to save up enough money to buy a car. Finally I had enough to buy an old used Dodge that looked like an overgrown beetle. I parked about a block from school because it was so ugly. My stepfather realized how ashamed I was to drive that old car to school, so he gave me his nice Ford to drive, and he drove my old Dodge to work. He was an incredible man.

After graduation my main goal in life was to join the police department. I liked the idea of "good guys" versus "bad guys," and the excitement and action of police work appealed to my sense of adventure. I explored the possibilities and discovered that if I enlisted in the Air Force, I could get into the Military Police and gain some experience in police work.

I've often wondered what direction my life might have taken had I joined the Navy before completing high school. My friend Bill went on to serve thirty years in the Navy; my cousin Jerry served and then became a police officer. I might have done something similar. I admit, I was extremely disappointed that Mom wouldn't sign the Naval permission form, but I'm deeply grateful today. Had I gone down that road, I would have missed so many wonderful opportunities. More importantly, I might have missed one of the most important spiritual moments of my life. The world-famous evangelist Billy Graham was coming to town for a crusade, and Mom wanted our family to attend.

The crusade was held at the LA Sports Arena, and the place was packed an hour before the service was scheduled to begin. People had come from all parts of Southern California to hear the straight-shooting preacher.

I was excited to go to the crusade, simply because it was such an enormous event, but I really didn't expect to experience anything of significance in my life as a result. After all, I had committed my life to Christ and had been baptized as a boy when our family attended Calvary Baptist Church. But this was different. This was pure power.

I listened to the beautiful music as Cliff Barrows led the mass choir, and the deep voice of soloist George Beverly Shea, and finally Billy Graham's powerful words; I felt a tugging on my heartstrings. The famous preacher explained that Christ had died on the cross in my place, that it really should have been me being punished by death for my sins. But Christ took my place. Now, by believing in him and believing that Jesus died and rose again from the dead, I could be forgiven of my sins, and I could be saved forever.

I listened intently, mesmerized by the words that were searing into my heart. When Billy Graham invited those in the Sports Arena who wanted to be forgiven of their sins and wanted to commit their lives to Jesus Christ to walk down to the front of the stage, I almost leapt to my feet. Had Mom, Weiland, and Aaron not wanted to go with me, I might have run down to the front.

Whether my response was an intellectual assent to the gospel or a recommitment to the faith I'd embraced as a child, I can't really say. All I know for sure is that from that night on, I knew my life was in God's hands. I believed, as Mom frequently reminded me (and still does!), that "God has plans for me."

I stood in the midst of about a thousand people as Mr. Graham explained God's plan of salvation. He then prayed a collective prayer for the large group of seekers. A counselor gave me some literature that clarified my decision and gave me some basic tips on how to study the Bible. We prayed together, and he encouraged me to go to church, which I was already doing. It was a rather simple, unemotional affair, but a very real transaction between God and me took place at the Arena that night. I committed myself to follow him, no matter what, and he committed himself to me as my Savior and Lord. Over the years I haven't always held up my end of the bargain, but — I'm thankful to say — he has never reneged on his.

In August 1958, two months after graduating from high school, I enlisted in the United States Air Force, with Mom's blessing. As soon as I signed the paperwork, the Air Force whisked me off to boot camp at Lackland Air Force Base in Texas. During boot camp, one of the guys in my barracks asked me about my name. "Carlos? That's a rather odd name for someone who isn't Hispanic, isn't it? What does Carlos mean in English?"

"It's roughly equivalent to Charles," I told him.

"Good, then we'll call you Chuck. Chuck Norris." The nickname has been with me ever since, although my family members and closest friends still call me Carlos.

For the next few months, I ate, drank, walked, talked, and slept military life. I didn't mind the rigorous workouts and training. In fact, as I started feeling stronger and in better physical condition, I began to develop a better sense of self-worth and confidence. I felt so good about the changes in my life, I decided to ask Dianne to marry me. I proposed to her in a letter, and she responded, "Yes!"

Dianne attended an Episcopal Church, so when I came home on leave four months later, she and I were married in a simple, traditional wedding ceremony in Torrance, California. I wore my Air Force uniform and Dianne looked radiant in her wedding gown. I was eighteen and Dianne had just turned seventeen.

Following a four-day honeymoon in Big Bear, California, Dianne moved to Arizona with me. We set up housekeeping just off the Air Force base in a twelve-foot-long trailer with no bathroom. We felt that we were living in luxury when we were finally able to move to an apartment with real plumbing. I was stationed at a base in Arizona for a year, and Dianne was able to remain with me. But then I was transferred to Osan, Korea. At nineteen I left behind my wife and stepped into an extremely uncertain future. The Korean War was over by then, but tensions still ran high between the newly divided countries of North Korea and South Korea. I had no way of knowing it then, but my stint in Korea was to become a major turning point in my life.

My military tour in Korea was the first time I had ever been out of the United States, and the poverty in the country was an eye-opener for me. I had grown up poor, but I had always had enough to eat. Yet many of the Koreans I saw were barely surviving on subsistence levels of food day after day. Life was a constant struggle for them, with no hope of improvement. More than ever before, I realized how fortunate I was to be an American. Until then I had taken for granted all the opportunities and benefits our great nation has to offer. I decided then and there I'd never make that mistake again.

At Osan Air Base soldiers could do three things with their spare time: (1) booze it up, (2) enroll in an academic class, or (3) study martial arts. I'd never been a drinker, and academic studies weren't my forte, so delving into the martial arts seemed the best way to pass the time.

Judo was the only martial art that I knew anything about, so I joined the judo club on the base. I was interested in learning something that would help me as a policeman when I left the service.

During my second week of judo training, I was practicing with another student, and he threw me. Rather than landing on my back, I fell directly on my shoulder. I heard a sickening crunching sound, and pain seared through my shoulder. Although I landed on the judo mat, I broke my collar bone in the awkward fall.

A few days later, with my arm in a sling, I went for a walk through the village of Osan with its straw huts and shabby market stalls. The strong aroma of kimchi (cabbage cooked with garlic) permeated the air and was almost overpowering in the narrow alleys.

As I walked through the village, I suddenly heard fierce yelling and saw people's heads popping up over the top of a knoll, like puppets on a string. Curious, I walked up to see what was going on. Several Koreans, dressed in what appeared to be white pajamas, were jumping up in the air and executing spectacular kicks. I had never before seen such incredible athletic maneuvers, and I could not believe that the human body was capable of such amazing feats. I stood there watching them for more than an hour, fascinated by the sight. I wanted to ask the Koreans what style of martial arts they were doing, but I was apprehensive about interrupting them.

When I returned to the base, I told my judo instructor, Mr. Ahn, what I had seen. "What kind of martial art is that?" I asked. "It's nothing like I've ever seen before!"

Mr. Ahn's lips hinted at a smile — he rarely smiled during class. "That style of Korean karate is called *tang soo do,* the art of empty-hand fighting, using your feet and hands as weapons."

"Do you think I could learn to do that?"

The judo instructor's face broke into a full-fledged smile. No wonder! I was only two weeks into learning judo! And I hadn't exactly been breaking any records with my progress. A broken collar bone? Yes. Nevertheless, Mr. Ahn was encouraging. "Yes, I believe you could learn *tang soo do,*" he said.

"Could I train in *tang soo do* while my shoulder is healing?" I asked.

"Oh, yes," the teacher responded. "It might be a good idea, although you must learn to block out the pain."

The next day Mr. Ahn took me into Osan Village to meet Mr. Jae Chul Shin (actually the Koreans place the last name first: Shin, Jae Chul), one of the instructors there. When I told Mr. Shin that I wanted to train with him, he looked skeptical. Americans had a sorry reputation for trying but not lasting long under the grueling training. And I was an American with a broken collar bone! What chance did I have of learning this highly physical martial art? Mr. Ahn convinced him to give me a shot.

There were twenty students in my class, most of whom were Korean black belts already! An unusual feature of the class was that everyone trained together, the beginners with the black belts. The theory was that if you wanted to learn, you learned, but no one actively encouraged you. The Koreans were not schooled in the psychology of teaching. Like most of the beginners, I struggled along, handicapped even further by my arm being in a sling. Still, I did most of the exercises with one arm. The black belts were indifferent to me, and I did my best to keep up with them.

The daily training sessions were five hours long, Monday through Saturday. My body was not limber, and the stretching exercises we did before each class were real agony. Classes started at 5:00 p.m., with five minutes rest between each hour.

For the first twenty minutes of each day's session, we warmed up by punching from a wide stationary stance. Then we practiced blocking techniques for forty minutes. For the next hour we practiced various kicks: front, side, round, and back. We spent the third hour working with a partner, with one attacking and the other attempting to block the attacker.

Then we reversed the procedure, with the partner who had earlier attacked doing the blocking and countering. Next we did those flying kicks that I had first seen and admired. For the fourth hour we did *heians*, choreographed movements fighting an imaginary opponent. During the final hour we free-sparred or fought against each other. It was the same routine day in and day out. It never varied, and it was especially difficult for me in the beginning since I had only one good arm, and no one was any easier on me because of my injury. Worse yet, compared to the other competitors, I was not in particularly good physical shape, nor was I especially well coordinated. But I was determined to learn *tang soo do,* so I refused to give up.

After my shoulder healed, I continued my daily classes in *tang soo do,* but I also studied judo for four hours every Sunday, my one day off from training in *tang soo do.* Many nights I went to bed so stiff and sore that I could hardly sleep. Despite the agony of training, I said to myself, "If I can stick with this, I can stick with anything!" I was learning discipline by developing the ability to do something that was never easy, not always pleasant, and about which I was not always enthusiastic. But I kept at it. I had not set my mind on achieving any particular goal, such as becoming a black belt. I just wanted to survive the training and perhaps learn some moves that might be helpful in my future career as a police officer.

Meanwhile I had my hands full with my job as an Air Force Military Policeman. The Koreans were resourceful people and had managed to illegally hook up the electricity for the entire village of Osan by tapping into a wire from our base. Every night the village would light up like a Christmas tree, powered by the US Air Force. Occasionally I drew the late shift, and it was my duty to drive around the perimeter of the base and locate the connection. When I found and removed the wires, the village would go totally dark. By the time I returned to headquarters to report, however, the village would be ablaze with lights again.

One of my daytime jobs was to guard the main gate and check the Korean workers as they left, since government property was constantly being "liberated." One day a *mamasan*, an elderly woman, who must have been seventy years old, approached the gate carrying a big bale of hay on her back. Before going through the gate, she sat down on a curb to rest. I noticed that when she tried to get up, she could not. I went over to help her up but was unable to heft the load. I started digging through the hay, and to my surprise found an entire Jeep engine hidden inside the bale! I confiscated it but soon regretted my decision. I couldn't begin to lift the thing! Five soldiers were needed to haul the engine back to the motor pool. How that little woman had been carrying it, I'll never know!

I continued studying *tang soo do* the entire time I was stationed in Osan. It took time for the Korean black belts to accept me, one of the few Caucasians in the class.

But when they saw how determined I was to learn and how willing I was to persevere no matter what the cost, they became friendlier. That didn't make the training any easier. Not being a natural athlete, developing strength and agility in the military was already a rough challenge for me. I had never before really stayed with any form of exercise or physical sports for long. Growing up, my tendency was to take the easy way, the convenient road of least resistance. I had a hard time sticking with anything. But the intense discipline I learned by studying the Korean form of karate inspired me. While the training caused my physical body to become more flexible, it infused steel into my spine and my spirit. I was determined to finish what I had started. I knew that I would never be the same, but I could never have dreamed that within eight years I would be sitting on top of the martial arts world as a champion!

CHAPTER 6

Cracking the Egg of Insecurity

Take a look at your hands. If you're a woman, you may use special creams to help keep your hands soft and beautiful. If you're an accountant, lawyer, secretary, or a person who spends most of the day nimbly typing at a computer, your hands may be more of a tool than a finely adorned extension of your arms. Construction workers, plumbers, and other manual-labor types often have rough, calloused hands.

Regardless, as you look at your hands, it may be hard to imagine them breaking through boards or bricks. Even more difficult, try imagining your hands as lethal weapons!

In *tang soo do,* great emphasis is placed on toughening up the hands in order to be able to break boards and bricks, the theory being that if you can hit hard enough to break a solid object, you can certainly damage an opponent. To build up calluses on my knuckles, I carried a flat rock with me everywhere I went, pounding my knuckles against the rock as I walked.

When I was in my third month of training, Mr. Shin announced that we were going to perform a demonstration in the village of Osan. The exhibition went well, and I survived relatively unscathed until near the end of the demonstration, when Mr. Shin stacked up eight roofing tiles. He looked around at our group. "You," he said, pointing to me. "You break!"

My heart began thumping wildly. I had never broken anything before. But I knew Mr. Shin would lose face in front of the villagers if I refused, so I crouched over the tiles and lined up two knuckles on top of the stack, just as Mr. Shin had taught us and as I'd seen some of the advanced students do. I took a deep breath and went for it! But somehow as my fist came down, I twisted my wrist, and instead of the two large knuckles buckling the tiles, the small knuckles in my hand took the force of the blow. I heard an awful crunching sound as my fist slammed down on the tiles. I broke the tiles, but I also broke my hand! Mr.

Shin was pleased, though. That was the Korean way of teaching: the student learns through trial and error.

As I got into better physical shape, my confidence continued to rise. For the first time in my life, I had stuck with something and had not given up. I was training both my body and my mind, and as a result of my discipline and learning, I was developing a much better self-image.

As I became more proficient in the martial arts, I carried myself differently, standing more erectly, walking and talking with an air of assurance. A few months after I started training, my new confidence began to show: I was chosen Airman of the Month by my company commanders.

I soon discovered, as a *tang so do* martial artist, that I was also a member of a very elite brotherhood whose members were extremely loyal to one another. One night a Korean air policeman who worked as an interpreter on the base was going home through an alley-type passageway. Like most alleys in Korea, it was so narrow that people had to turn sideways to pass each other. Suddenly he was jumped by surprise by six *slicky* boys (young Korean muggers). One of the attackers had a knife.

Contrary to images portrayed by martial

arts movies, including my own, knowing karate or some other martial art does not make a person invincible. The air policeman avoided the knife attack, but in the confined, cramped conditions, he couldn't kick and was unable to maneuver well, especially against the muggers coming at him from various directions in the dark. The ambushers beat him up badly and robbed him.

The air policeman was a black belt in *tang soo do*. When the *slicky* boys found this out, they were so horrified at the potential reprisal they might suffer, they printed an apology in the local paper. It did them no good. When somebody messes with one black belt, he or she is challenging the whole organization. One of our members tracked down several of the attackers. He killed one and injured two. The police arrested him, and he was sentenced to three years in prison. He was back out on the street in two weeks. The lesson was clear: Mess with one member of our group, and you are messing with all.

After almost a year of daily practice, Mr. Shin told me I was ready for my black belt test. Now every move I made during training was observed by critical eyes. Mr. Shin and the other black belts mercilessly drilled me over and over on the various techniques on which I might be tested, and that I had already practiced to exhaustion hundreds of times. Every technique I had learned was sharpened by constant, loudly shouted, cutting remarks. The Korean teaching method tends to focus on what a student is doing wrong rather than on what he or she is doing well.

I was a nervous and physical wreck by the time I was scheduled to face the board of examiners in Seoul. My sergeant let me borrow a Jeep from the motor pool for the forty-mile drive to Seoul. It was the dead of winter, the roads were icy, and the drive took two hours. The Jeep's heater provided negligible warmth, and I arrived stiff with cold at the *dojang* (training hall) where the test was to be held.

The *dojang* was a big unheated building with wind blowing through open spaces in the walls. It was freezing inside as well as out. I changed into my *gi*, my white karate uniform, and sat down cross-legged on the bare wooden floor, along with the other people testing. I was the only student from my school among two hundred strangers testing for various ranks. The board of examiners sat stone-faced at a table.

I watched as the others exhibited their

forms and free-sparred with selected black belts. At first I passed the time by comparing myself to the other novices, whom I watched with great interest. Within half an hour, however, my mind could focus only on how cold and stiff I was from sitting on the floor waiting to test. After about three hours of sitting, my body was numb. Then I heard my name called.

I uncrossed my legs and stood, still a bit wobbly from sitting in one position for so long. I walked over to the examiners, bowed, and heard someone tell me in Korean to do the form *bassai*. *Bassai* was the final form a student must learn to qualify for the black belt exam. It was similar to a choreographed dance except that it involved displaying various defenses against an opponent in an imaginary fight. Although I had done the routine countless times before, my mind suddenly went blank. I could not, for the life of me, remember how to do the *bassai*. As a comparison, imagine taking ballroom dance lessons for months and learning all sorts of steps, twirls, and routines, but then at your recital you could not remember the most rudimentary of moves. That is how I felt. My concentration had been broken by the cold and my nervousness. After a few embarrassing moments, I confessed to the examiners that I could not remember the form.

"Go sit down," one of the examiners said, barely concealing the disdain in his voice. I returned to my spot on the cold floor, where I sat for the next four hours, until the other students finished testing. I had already failed the examination, but to get up and leave before the others completed their test would be disrespectful and disobedient to the examiner's orders and would have effectively ended my martial arts career.

I sat, fuming over my failure on the inside and freezing on the outside. Those four hours seemed like the longest four hours of my life.

I was miserable on the drive back to the base. Over and over again I thought about the form I had forgotten. Still frustrated and angry with myself, I knew I had to put the failure out of my mind. If I continued to dwell on it, I would be setting myself up to fail again. I had to prepare to succeed, and I had to begin planting those seeds immediately.

Mr. Shin said nothing about my failing the test. It was almost as if the exam never happened. He didn't scold or belittle me for my mental lapse. He simply plowed back into a vigorous training program. I trained for an additional three months before he said I was ready to take the exam again. By then I had put the first failure out of my mind and visualized myself doing perfectly any form that was requested. I played out in my mind the scenario for any exhibition the examiners might come up with. More importantly, I saw myself completing the test successfully.

The test was just as grueling as the previous one, but this time I was ready when my name was called. I did my forms, some one-step punching and board breaking; then I free-sparred against a black belt. Everything went as I had visualized it in my mind.

A few weeks later Mr. Shin took me aside after class. Smiling broadly, he told me, "You have passed the black belt exam." He bowed formally and presented me with a new black belt with my name written on it in Korean, as well as a silver pin designating my black belt rank to be worn on my lapel. That pin was soon to take on a special significance for me.

One night while I was walking in the village wearing my civvies, five *slicky* boys stopped me in an alley. I was about to take them on when they saw the pin on my lapel. Their eyes widened in fear, and they ran off. I felt like Clark Kent wearing his Superman costume!

Earning my black belt changed my life in many ways. I had accomplished something difficult on my own. Being a *shodan* (first degree black belt) was like getting a college degree. Belt ranks are like school levels, starting with elementary school (white belt) and proceeding to different colors, depending on the martial arts style, similar to advancing through junior high, high school, and college.

By the end of my tour of duty in the Air Force, I was a first-degree black belt in *tang soo do*, and a third-degree brown belt in judo. I had also been promoted to the rank of airman first class.

The Air Force had provided the opportunity for me to learn much about the martial arts. Now the martial arts would help me learn much about life.

CHAPTER 7

Karate Kick-off

It's almost impossible for a civilian who has never served in the military to comprehend fully the toll that extended service to our country can take on a young married couple. Military life is tough enough on a family, even in the best of circumstances, and the strain is exacerbated when couples are separated by continents for long periods of time.

Upon completing my tour of duty in Korea, I was reassigned to March Air Force Base in Riverside, California. I had a thirty-day leave before I needed to report, and I looked forward to getting reacquainted with my young wife. Dianne had rented a small apartment on the outskirts of the Air Force base when she had learned that I'd be coming home. She busied herself decorating and getting our home ready for us, while I made the transition from

Korea, to Tokyo, to San Francisco.

When I arrived in San Francisco, I was flat broke. I needed to call Dianne to let her know that I'd be landing in Los Angeles later that same day, but I had only nine cents in my pocket. At that time most pay phones required a dime to make even a collect call. With less than two minutes before my plane closed its doors, I finally found someone who would give me a dime in exchange for my nine cents. I quickly dialed the number and told Dianne that I was on my way home!

Reestablishing my relationship with Dianne, however, proved to be more difficult than I'd anticipated. Like many military couples, we had married young, and now, after having been apart for more than a year while I'd been in Korea, we both had changed, matured in many ways, and become disenchanted in others. Although Dianne and I had communicated regularly by mail throughout my absence, resuming ordinary, day-to-day life together was extremely stressful. It soon became obvious that not only had we been physically separated; we had grown apart in our relationship, as well.

Nevertheless, we were determined to hold our marriage together. We consciously worked at restoring our relationship, starting by getting to know each other again. It wasn't easy, but we worked through the readjustment period and came out stronger for it. Undoubtedly, part of my willingness to stick to it was a direct result of the perseverance I had learned through my instruction in *tang soo do*.

Back home I continued practicing *tang soo do* on my own, using a large tree in front of our house as a punching bag. Whenever I passed by, I stopped to pound on it for a few minutes to keep my knuckles hard and callused. Passersby who spotted me punching a tree must have thought I was nuts!

Japanese Karate was becoming a well-known martial art in the United States in the early 1960s, but no karate classes existed at the base, so I found a judo club and joined immediately. I began competing in matches and won enough to earn a trip to Seattle, Washington, for the 15th Division Air Force Judo Championships. In judo, competitors are matched by weight, not by rank. About forty of us in my weight division, ranging from white belts (beginners) to black belts, all competed against one another. I beat three black belts and made it into the semifinals along with two black belts and a white belt.

Before my next match, I hoped I would be lucky enough to draw the white belt as my opponent. I was confident I could beat him and then go on to the finals. We drew numbers from a basket to determine the matchups, and I got my wish! I drew the white belt.

In my mind I had already won the match with him. After all, I had beaten three black belts. But I had forgotten that my opponent had gotten to the top the same way. When we got on the mat, I expected an easy win but soon found I was in a real battle, one that I eventually lost. After the match I congratulated my opponent and told him he was one of the strongest men I had ever encountered.

"I'm a lumberjack by trade," he explained.

"Now I know why trying to move you around was like trying to move an oak tree," I said.

In addition to competing in judo matches, I kept practicing *tang soo do* by myself at the base. One day a couple of GIs saw me doing some kicks. They were intrigued and asked me to teach them. I went through the proper military channels and received permission to start a karate club on the base, using the auditorium as a training area. I didn't mention *tang soo do*, but simply used the more familiar term *karate* instead because everyone had at least heard of karate, and few if any had any knowledge of *tang soo do.*

At the opening meeting of the karate club, I planned to put on a demonstration and give a little talk. I wasn't worried about the martial arts portion of my program, but I was scared stiff to stand up and speak in public. Although I was twenty-one years old, the thought of speaking before an audience still terrified me. I decided to write a speech and memorize it. I wrote out what I wanted to say and then tape-recorded myself reading it. I listened to the tape for hours, repeating the speech over and over. Finally, I had it down pat.

A few hundred people gathered in the auditorium that night: soldiers, officers, and their families. I was sweating profusely from the tension of having to speak. I gathered my courage, walked up to the microphone, and said, "Good evening ladies and gentleman. My name is Chuck Norris, and I would like to welcome you here tonight. . . ."

That's the last thing I remember. The

next thing I knew I was walking to the center of the auditorium to do my demonstration. I was thinking, *Did I finish my speech or just lay the microphone down?* To this day I still don't know, but at least the martial arts had given me the strength to crack the egg of insecurity that I had carried around for twenty-one years. I kept forcing myself to speak to groups in public gatherings until it was no longer a problem for me.

The karate club at the Air Force base became a huge success. My students got into such excellent physical shape that they scored highest of all the soldiers on the base in the physical fitness tests. That raised the stature of our club significantly in the eyes of the military brass. The more successful we became, the more cooperation we received. Lieutenant General Archie J. Old, the 15th Division Air Force commander, even joined our club and became an honorary black belt.

I was assigned to Stead Air Force Base in Reno, Nevada, for ten weeks of combat training, along with sixty other GIs from all over the country, most of whom had been trained as military police or intelligence officers. Every day we studied four hours of classroom work and four hours of physical training in karate, judo, knife-fighting, and *jujitsu*. Before long, I was tapped to teach the karate class, and at the end of the course, I won the Outstanding Student Award.

Altogether I spent four years in the Air Force, and my training proved invaluable to me. I matured as a man and will always be grateful to, and appreciative of, the US military. Nevertheless, I was looking forward to beginning my new career as a police officer. That had been my goal upon entering the Air Force, and now I felt ready for a job in the Los Angeles Police Department. Unfortunately, they weren't ready for me. Job openings in the field of law enforcement were scarce in Los Angeles at the time. Dianne was eight months pregnant, so I decided I'd have to seek other employment until something opened up in my career of choice.

Soon after I was discharged from the Air Force in 1962, my stepfather arranged an interview for me at Northrop Aircraft, the defense contractor where he worked. I was hired as a file clerk in records management for a salary of $320 a month. Two months later my son Mike was born.

Although the desk job was not to my liking, I was grateful for it. I had a wife and a child to support and was glad to be bringing home a weekly paycheck. Sometimes you have to do whatever you can while you're searching for something better. In the meantime I prepared to join the Los Angeles Police Department, but there was a six-month waiting list of qualified applicants. Looking back now, it's easy to see that what I then considered a delay and a detour was actually preparation time. God was getting me ready to travel a different path than the one I thought I'd be pursuing. Had I gone directly to work for the LAPD, I'd probably be a law enforcement officer yet today. That would have been fine with me, but as Mom said, "God had plans for me," and apparently his plans were not the same as my own! Had I not encountered the "obstacle" in my career path, I might never have become a karate champion, nor would I have pursued a career in movies and television.

To supplement my income from Northrop, I began teaching karate in my parents' backyard after work. My first students were my brothers — Aaron, who was nine years old, and Wieland, who was nineteen. I had begun teaching them when I first came back from Korea, so we simply picked up where we had left off.

Soon word began to spread around the neighborhood about the Norris brothers, three fair-haired boys doing karate. We started getting invitations from the Rotary Club and other civic organizations to put on martial arts demonstrations. Aaron was a cute kid, so we had a demonstration in which he threw us "big guys" around. Audiences loved it. So did Aaron, at least for the first five or six demonstrations. By then he decided he'd had enough.

When the Kiwanis Club called and asked us to put on a demonstration, Wieland was agreeable, but Aaron said he didn't want to participate with us anymore. I insisted, and Aaron went along. He cried all the way to the club, but after we started our routine, he got into it.

The response to our demonstrations revealed that people were far more interested in karate, which was still relatively new in the United States, than I ever realized. With Dianne's blessing I decided to delay joining the police department so I could try teaching professionally. I opened my first karate school in Torrance, California, a Los Angeles suburb. The "studio" was a fifteen-by-thirty-foot storefront at the intersection of two main streets. My stepfather cosigned for a loan of $600, enough for the first month's rent, mats for the floor, two big mirrors on the walls, and a fresh coat of paint. My "office" was a tiny desk in a corner. The entire family pitched in to paint the store, which was soon transformed into a studio. We even hand-lettered a sign to read "Chuck Norris Karate" and hung it outside.

The school turned out to be something of a traffic hazard. As cars passed by, they would slow down to look through the windows at the classes. Some of the passersby became interested in what we were doing and eventually signed up for classes. More than a few gawkers simply slammed into the cars in front of them.

I started with ten students who paid ten dollars each per month, entitling them to three classes per week. Keeping up with even that small group of students was no small feat. For the next two years, I continued to work at Northrop from 8:00 a.m. to 5:00 p.m. weekdays. I'd hurry home, gulp dinner down, and then race to the studio where I would teach from 6:00 p.m. to 10:00 p.m. That routine rarely changed. It was an exhausting schedule, and Dianne and I began to dream of the day when I'd have enough students to quit my job at Northrop. After teaching in Torrance for a year, I had thirty students, and raised my fees to $15 per month, which gave me an additional $450 per month gross on top of my income from Northrop. My goal was to have sixty students.

The more I taught, the more I realized how much I enjoyed teaching. After discussing the risks with Dianne, I decided to give up my plan to become a police officer and become a full-time martial arts instructor.

By 1964, our karate teaching business had grown to the point that I employed several assistant instructors. I was running myself ragged, so I decided to leave my secure job at Northrop, a frightening step. I opened a second school in Redondo Beach and soon realized that in order to recruit more students, we needed more advertising. But on our shoestring budget, we really couldn't afford to lay out money for publicity. Mulling over our predicament, I thought, *If I could compete in and win a karate tournament, I might get a write-up in a karate magazine or in the local paper.* That would attract attention to our schools and bring in more students.

I entered a karate tournament, but the results were not what I had planned.

CHAPTER 8

Becoming a Champion

In most professional sports a competitor in his early twenties is considered in the prime of life. But even in amateur karate ranks, at twenty-four years of age, I was already older than most of my opponents in the high energy, demanding martial arts competitions. Nevertheless, in 1964 I entered my first karate tournament in Salt Lake City, Utah. I drove there from Los Angeles with three of my students, who also planned to compete. The trip took sixteen hours in my old Ford Falcon, and we almost didn't make it because of a snowstorm we encountered along the way.

We arrived a few hours before the tournament was to begin. I warmed up with my students, all of whom were in the beginner and intermediate division. I weighed in at a pound and a half over the black belt lightweight division, which meant that I'd be fighting as one of the lightest middleweight black belts. I knew I shouldn't have had that big breakfast!

In those days competitors in amateur karate tournaments fought bare fisted and barefooted. We were allowed to inflict medium contact to the body but no contact to the face. At the professional levels light contact is allowed without being penalized unless a fighter intentionally tries to hurt his opponent, in which case he is punished by a loss of points.

Obviously, "accidents" sometimes happen in karate matches, but that is not the intent of the competition. For instance, during my competitive years, I had my nose broken three times, cracked several bones in my body, and endured an untold number of bruises. During the competitions I hardly felt a thing because of the enormous rush of adrenaline, but, oh, the next morning when I tried to get out of bed. . . .

When my name was called to begin my first tournament, I stepped into the fighting area, similar in size to a boxing ring. The matches were officiated by a center referee who was assisted by four side judges, one at each corner of the ring. Each judge had a red flag in one hand and a white flag in the other; each contestant wore either a white or a red ribbon on his belt. The colored flags and ribbons were used for scoring.

A point was given for an *ippon* (a "killing" blow), a single-focused attack, not deflected or blocked, that landed directly on a vital area of the body. It had to be delivered with good form and balance, proper distance and explosive but controlled force. When a point was scored, the judges held up a red or white flag to indicate which fighter had earned it. Three of the five judges had to have seen a scoring blow for it to be awarded.

All of this was new and confusing to me. I had never before fought under such formal conditions, and I had little time to get acclimated to the rules and procedures.

My first match was with a man I knew, a fighter from Colorado, who had also been in the military in Korea. We took up our starting positions in the center of the ring. On the command *hajime,* "Begin!" given by the center judge, we engaged and threw ourselves into the battle. Each of us tried to penetrate the other's defenses. I recall little about that first fight or the one that followed, other than the fact that I won. There was no time for elation, however. After a brief rest, it was time to fight again!

My third fight was with a well-known Hawaiian fighter. My best and only weapons were my kicks. The Hawaiian had watched carefully how I had beaten my first two opponents, and once in the ring he took steps to counter my best moves. He beat me with a punch.

The matches were hotly contested, but when the smoke from the heavy competition cleared, my three students had won and I had lost. I was still smarting within as I drove all the way back to Los Angeles, my students clinging to their trophies and exuberantly reliving the highlights of their victorious matches. Meanwhile I mulled over how I had lost. I decided then and there, *I may lose another tournament, but I'll never lose the same way twice.*

I went back to the studio to train, determined to find out what I was doing wrong. I was so upset with myself that on the first night of training, I worked out so hard I lost six pounds! OK, it was mostly water weight, but my students dropped an average of four to five pounds that night, too, thanks to the vigorous workout I led us through.

The next scheduled tournament was the Internationals, held in Long Beach, California. It was the largest amateur karate tournament in the world, with more than three thousand fighters entered. I fought in the middleweight division and lost again.

Rather than being dejected, I continued training with increased vigor, concentrating on my weak points: I had to improve my timing; I had to learn to close the space between my opponent and me more quickly; and I had to develop more confidence as a fighter. I also worked on perfecting some of the techniques I had learned in Korea, including the spinning back kick. I felt I could use it effectively in future contests because I could perform the move fairly well while it was still unfamiliar to many Americans.

In May 1964, our second son, Eric, was born. I was thrilled with our new baby, but I was obsessed with winning a karate tournament. As soon as we brought Eric home from the hospital, I threw myself back into my training. A few days later I entered Tak Kubota's All-Stars Tournament in Los Angeles.

In those days the point system for scoring varied according to the tournament and the region in which the match was held. In some matches the winner was the first contestant to score two points; in others the contestant who scored the most points in the allotted time won the match. In the All-Stars Tournament, a match lasted two minutes; the fighter with the most points at the end of that time was the winner. The Japanese judges, all senior black belts themselves, were stingy with points. Unless a technique was flawless, they usually awarded only a half point.

I made it to the finals and was feeling quite confident until I learned that the man contending for the championship was Ron Marchini. An American who fought in the Japanese style, Ron stood about five foot nine inches tall, had a closely cropped batch of blonde hair, and was known as a strong, tough competitor.

Our match began, and we approached each other cautiously, knowing that one careless move could cost the championship. Neither of us was able to score on the other until about halfway into the match, when Ron feinted a kick but unexpectedly followed through with a stepping punch that I attempted to block.

Too late! His timing and control were superb. I could feel his knuckle prints on my solar plexus. Three of the side judges held out their white flags horizontally to signal a half point for Ron.

The match restarted, and Ron began to fight defensively, holding onto his lead, as the time ticked away. I glanced at the clock and saw that just fifteen seconds remained. I attacked, grabbed Ron's *gi,* swept his feet out from under him, and punched him in the ribs. I followed up with a *shuto* (edge of the hand) chop to the neck just as the buzzer went off, signaling the end of the fight. Four judges held their red flags up vertically to indicate that I had scored an *ippon* (full point). I had won the championship by half a point!

It was my first win and a high point in my life. The satisfaction of knowing that I had finally won a tournament increased my confidence and motivated me to continue competing. More importantly, as I had hoped, my increased visibility also increased the number of students wanting to learn karate in my schools.

Next I set my sights on the California state title. I went to the tournament with twelve of my students, ranging from white belts to black belts. I won the Middle-weight Championship with my spinning back kick, a move that was rapidly becoming my trademark and most effective weapon. But I lost the Grand Championship. Eleven of my twelve students won their matches, and the Norris School dominated the tournament!

The matchups for the first fight are often determined by who is standing next to you, so before long, when other competitors saw the school patch on our *gi*, they would attempt to reposition themselves in the line to avoid having to fight a Norris student first. Our students took that as a compliment, and so did I!

In 1965, I entered and won several tournaments, including the Winter Nationals in San Jose, California. I became a major championship competitor by again defeating Ron Marchini for the Grand Champion title. That win encouraged me to set my sights on the Internationals, the most prestigious of all the tournaments.

I won the middleweight division of the 1966 Internationals by defeating a fighter who had beaten me the year before. That win felt great. But the feeling didn't last long; my fight for the Grand Championship was with Allen Steen, a big fellow from Dallas, Texas, who had long legs with tremendous power and knew how to use his height to his advantage. He had just defeated Joe Lewis, one of the best of the new fighters, and I thought, *Anyone who can beat Joe must be really good.* I was right. I lost to Allen too. I decided to take some time off, to recoup, and to prepare for a heavy tournament schedule in 1967.

I realized that although I had gotten good results with the spinning back kick in my first few tournaments, my opponents were now anticipating it. To be able to compete effectively in future matches, I would have to increase my repertoire. At that time, most karate fighters were either good kickers or good with their hands, but few of them could blend kicks and punches together.

Many of my friends were top martial arts instructors. Normally it is difficult to go from one karate studio to another to train because each style is different, but several of my instructor friends allowed me to train with them.

Fumio Demura, the 1963 All-Japan Karate Champion and an expert in *shito ryu,* showed me how to blend moves, using my hands and feet together, to create a more varied arsenal of kicks and punches. I learned hand-and-foot combinations from Hidetaka Nishiyama, a master of *shotokan* karate.

Tutamu Ohshima, another *shotokan*

master, encouraged me to go beyond my physical limitations. He pushed me to the point where I didn't think I could do any more, and then he encouraged me to go even further!

Jun Chung, a master of *hapkido,* a martial art that emphasizes kicks and throws, helped me perfect more Korean techniques. *Jujitsu* instructor Al Thomas worked with me on grappling techniques. Ed Parker, the father of American *kenpo* karate (a Chinese martial art) and promoter of the Internationals, spent hours in his studio teaching me his system. I also trained with Gene LeBell, an expert in wrestling, boxing, judo, and karate. Gene is one of the toughest men I know.

All of these men were generous with their time and talent. It says a great deal about the martial arts community that, although we were competitors from various styles and I'd possibly be an opponent to some of their students, we were all willing to share our knowledge.

I took something from each style and modified it for myself, incorporating the new skills into what I already knew. Soon I had such a variety of techniques, I was confident that an opponent would find it almost impossible to pinpoint a specific movement and zero in on it.

Joe Lewis, one of the up-and-coming fighters in the country, moved from North Carolina to Los Angeles. He called one day and asked if he could come to my school and spar with me. "Sure, Joe. Come on over," I told him. "You're more than welcome at our place." A natural athlete and a weight lifter, Joe had earned his black belt after only seven months of training during his stint with the Marine Corp in Okinawa. Joe entered his first tournament — the National Karate Championship — with less than two years of training under his belt, and he won it.

When Joe and I first began sparring together, I could score on him quite easily. But after a couple of months of sparring regularly, I found it extremely difficult to score a point on him. I quipped to my black belt students, "It may have been a mistake to spar with Joe so often because one day I am going to have to fight him in competition!"

My prediction soon became a reality when I was invited to fight in a Tournament of Champions in New York City. The top ten fighters in the United States were to fight a round-robin, a tournament in which every fighter competes against every other fighter. The competitor with the most victories would be the champion.

Joe Lewis was one of the ten, and the decisive fight came down to Joe and me. We had beaten everyone else, and now we would face each other to decide the championship.

Joe's two principal weapons were a lightning-fast side kick and a quick and powerful back fist. A smart and intimidating fighter, Joe instinctively understood what the Japanese refer to as *kyo* (weakness), and he looked for that in his opponent.

To beat Joe I knew I'd have to be aggressive from the start and force him to think defensively rather than offensively. I was in top physical shape, I had my techniques down pat, and my reflexes were sharp. I was also psychologically determined to win, but I knew this was going to be a tough fight.

Joe and I bowed to start the march. As I stepped into a fighting stance, Joe immediately drilled me with a side kick. Ouch! Joe was awarded one point, jumping out to a quick lead. The match began again, and I counterattacked, scoring with a reverse punch. After that, neither one of us could score on the other. We went into three overtimes and still neither of us could score! The judges decided they would have to make a decision on the winner. They awarded me the victory because I had been more aggressive in the match. It was a match that Joe and I would relive many times in the future.

CHAPTER 9

When Warriors Collide

Hundreds of karate fighters from all over the world gathered at Madison Square Garden in New York to compete in the 1967 All-American Karate Championship. I arrived in New York the night before the tournament and went to bed early. I knew from experience that it was important to have a good night's sleep so I would be totally relaxed on the day of the fight. But when I got into bed, my mind was racing. Usually, if I'm having a hard time falling asleep, I'll imagine that I am watching a movie screen that suddenly goes black. For some reason the mental exercise relaxes me, and I can drift off to sleep while waiting for the "movie" to come on again. That's what I did the night before the karate championship in New York. I awoke on the morning of the tournament completely refreshed.

When I arrived at the Garden, I saw all the other competitors standing around, talking to old friends, joking and laughing. A strong camaraderie exists among karate fighters. If I hadn't known better, it would have been hard to imagine that we were all warriors about to do battle.

I went to the locker room, took my freshly laundered uniform from my overnight bag, undressed, and stashed my clothes in a locker. My *gi* felt comfortable, almost as though it was a part of my body. It had become my favorite clothing, loose in the shoulders, with sleeves and pants that snapped like a whip when I kicked or punched.

I took deep breaths, exhaling slowly, attempting to keep myself relaxed and in a calm state. I knew that tension or stress burns energy. I wanted to be totally relaxed prior to fighting, conserving the energy that I would need when I stepped into the ring.

The tournament director called the black belts in the middleweight division to line up for pairing. I went straight to the middle of the floor and let the line form on each side of me. Some of the black belts hung back to scout the opposition. They were trying to pick their opponents so they wouldn't have to exert themselves too strenuously in the early matches.

The various competitors — lightweights, middleweights, light heavyweights, and heavyweights — were to fight in different rings. The winners of the respective weight divisions would then fight each other. The Grand Champion would be the man who defeated the winners of all the other weight divisions!

I settled down on the sidelines to watch the other black belts compete. Now that I had become tournament wise, it was a matter of routine for me to study the other competitors. I knew that I might have to confront some of them later on. I watched the way the fighters walked for signs of injury. I observed the way they stretched and warmed up: a kicker warms up with kicks and combinations of kicks, usually working on the one he will use most when under pressure. A fighter with good hand techniques warms up with repetitions and the combinations he favors.

I studied the losers as well as the winners. The winners were the ones I would probably have to fight. The losers were men I might have to fight in the future. The techniques that fighters implemented, especially the ones with which they scored most often, were my immediate concerns.

I didn't simply observe the winners and losers. I visualized myself in the ring with whichever man I was watching. I studied his strengths and his weaknesses; I inventoried my own techniques and matched them to his defenses. I visualized myself taking his strengths from him while maintaining my own. If, for example, I could see myself blocking an opponent's powerful side kick and then scoring with my own technique, I knew I would be able to do it when the real match began.

In competition, as in attempting to reach any goal in life, it's necessary to keep a "big picture" mentality, but the focus must be on the next step, the immediate goal at hand. When I was competing, I took the matches one at a time, concentrating my full energy on the match in which I was competing, not on the Grand Championship. I knew the priority was to beat my first opponent.

On this day in 1967, I had trained hard, my reflexes were razor sharp, and I was in peak physical and mental condition. I knew what I was going to do against each opponent because I had already visualized my match with each of them in my mind, and I knew their strengths and weaknesses.

As the tournament progressed, one of the top contenders who emerged was Hiroshi Nakamura, the All-Japan Middleweight champion. I sat on the sidelines watching as Mr. Nakamura methodically eliminated his opponents. A small, powerfully built man, Mr. Nakamura had moves that were smooth and polished, but all of a similar pattern. His specialty was a front kick produced with blinding speed, followed by a straight punch delivered as easily and quickly as a snap of the fingers, only with enormous power.

I studied him carefully, and I noticed that when I was in the ring, he sat at ringside scrutinizing me. But I had an edge on him; I had studied the Japanese styles of karate, as well as the Korean. I knew what he knew, but he didn't know what I knew!

Mr. Nakamura wound up winning his division, and I won mine, which meant that after dinner that night, we would face each other for the Middleweight Championship.

Before dinner I stopped by the washroom. Who should I see but my after-dinner opponent! I approached him and said, "Good luck tonight, Mr. Nakamura."

"I think you are going to beat me," he said bluntly.

His surprisingly negative attitude took me off guard, and I found myself encouraging my competition. "No, you've got a good chance," I said. "I've been watching you, and you are very good."

Regardless of what I told him, I knew I could beat him because I had already visualized the bout in my mind and was prepared for his attacks. I was also ready for his defenses. Despite this mental exercise of visualization and psyching-up before a bout, there were times when I didn't win, but I always believed that I would.

Nakamura and I chatted amiably for a few minutes. Normally, I never minded talking to anyone before a contest. No matter what I was doing — having dinner, getting dressed, or wrapping my hands before a fight — I was happy to have a conversation. But this carefree attitude changed instantly once I stepped into the ring. Then my concentration was totally on the task at hand: winning. I am not by nature an aggressive person, but I was superaggressive in the ring.

Even my martial arts students were sometimes amazed at the transformation that came over me when the competition turned serious. During class at our studio, I sparred with my black belt students, and often one or more of them would beat me. "Mr. Norris, I don't understand," a student might complain. "I can beat you in class but never in a real competition."

I'd smile and say, "Because in class I'm focused on teaching, not on winning; but in the ring, when I'm facing an opponent, my whole attitude changes. I am focused on winning!"

There are three facets to being a winner: mental, psychological, and physical. I prepare myself mentally by knowing my competitor's strengths and weaknesses and how I can take advantage of both. When I am mentally sharp, I'm aware of and see everything that goes on around me. I prepare psychologically by believing in my ability and knowing that I can win. I prepare physically by being in the best possible shape, able to execute my techniques to the best of my ability. When I am at the top of my form, I often hit an opponent even before my brain records it. I see an opening and go for it.

A winner must have a positive attitude. He visualizes himself scoring the winning points, and he sees the referee raising his hand in victory. These positive images create the will and the impetus to succeed. But having a positive image is worthless unless you are psychologically, physically, and mentally prepared to win.

I went back to Madison Square Garden after dinner for the finals. I put on my *gi*, and, as I usually did, I taped my big toes to the ones next to them with adhesive-tape, to help prevent injuries that often result from hard kicks.

The tournament rules called for each match to be two minutes long. The fighter who had scored the most points when the time expired was the winner.

When my name and Mr. Nakamura's were called over the loudspeaker, I stepped into the ring. The Garden was filled with thousands of screaming fans. The roar of the fans sounded to me like a waterfall thundering in the distance. Everyone was anticipating a great fight.

The moment I stepped into the ring, I forced myself to relax by slowing down my breathing. It's difficult to move when you're tense; relaxed muscles collaborate with rather than contradict each other, and I knew I could move faster when relaxed.

Since I had already visualized the entire fight in my mind, my strategy was to take away Mr. Nakamura's strong techniques. I was certain that his first move was going to be his front kick. I was right, although his kick came faster than I had anticipated. I had to respond quickly. The moment he started to move, I shifted aside, blocked the kick, and hit him in the stomach, scoring a point!

I expected his next attack would be another front kick followed by a punch. Again I was right. He snapped the kick, and I shifted to the right away from it. As he threw the punch, I blocked and countered with my own punch which scored again!

In those days, when Japanese stylists kicked, they never faked or feinted. Their kicks went straight to the intended target. They were not accustomed to someone faking a kick to one area and landing it elsewhere. Knowing this, I faked a kick to the stomach. As Mr. Nakamura started to block, I shifted my kick to his head and scored another point! I scored regularly enough to wind up beating him 12 to 1 for the Middleweight Championship.

After that bout I fought the lightweight champion and won. Next I was scheduled to fight the heavyweight champion who had beaten the light heavyweight champion. He was none other than Joe Lewis, whom I would have to fight for the second time in four months for the Grand Championship.

Joe had breezed through his competition and looked totally relaxed and rested. We stepped into the ring, stared at each other and bowed. The referee shouted *hajime!* The fight was on, and it was fast and furious. Joe jumped out in front by nailing me early with a side kick to my ribs. After that it was a fight to the finish. I finally scored on him to tie the match, then just as time was running out, I caught him again with a back fist to the face. When the dust cleared, I had won the match by one point and was awarded the All-American Grand Championship trophy.

I was almost too exhausted to celebrate my victory. I had been fighting since eight o'clock that morning and had faced thirteen strong, agile opponents in eleven hours. All I wanted was a hot shower and a good night's sleep.

But as I was leaving the stadium, Bruce Lee, one of the best-known martial artists in the world at that time, came over to congratulate me. I knew of Bruce, but we had never met. I had seen him put on a terrific demonstration at the Internationals in 1964, and I was familiar with his work as an actor on the *Green Hornet* television series.

Bruce was extremely complimentary of

my skills, recognizing what a feat it had been to snatch the victory away from Joe in the final moments of the Grand Championship. We talked amiably for a while, and after discovering that we were staying at the same hotel, we walked back together, talking all the way about martial arts and our philosophies. We were still deeply involved in conversation as the elevator whisked us up to our rooms. We stopped on Bruce's floor, and I stepped out with him.

It was already close to midnight, but we were so engrossed in our conversation, we continued exchanging martial arts techniques right there in the hallway! The next time I looked at my watch, it was 4:00 a.m.! We had worked out together for four hours! Bruce was so dynamic that it had seemed like only twenty minutes. It's a wonder that someone didn't call hotel security about the two maniacs out there tossing each other around in the hotel hallway!

Not long after that, Bruce invited me to work out with him in the backyard of his home in Culver City, California. Bruce had all sorts of training equipment out in the yard, including a wooden practice dummy — complete with sticks for arms, legs, and feet — that looked as though he'd made it himself, a straw-padded striking post to practice punches, padded chest protectors, and boxing gloves. We trained twice a week for three or four hours per session. Bruce taught me some of his trademark *kung fu* techniques, and in turn I taught him some high-kicking *tae kwon do* moves. Bruce had never believed in kicking above the waist, but when I demonstrated some high spinning heel kicks, he was intrigued. Within six months he could perform the high kicks as well as I could and added them to his repertoire with tremendous proficiency. Bruce was an extremely capable and knowledgeable martial artist and, pound for pound, one of the strongest men I've ever known.

His strongest attribute and his greatest fault, perhaps, were one and the same: Bruce Lee lived and breathed the martial arts. He turned even the most mundane, ordinary aspects of life into some sort of training. I'm not certain he ever knew how to relax.

We became good friends, close enough for him to share his dream with me. "Chuck, I want to be a film star," he told me. "Everything I do is a stepping-stone toward that goal." Indeed, Bruce was already teaching martial arts to a number of private students, including NBA basketball great, Kareem Abdul-Jabbar, and several high-profile Hollywood film stars, such as James Coburn, Lee Marvin, and Steve McQueen. His students often recommended Bruce for work in films, and Bruce had worked as a stunt coordinator on several. But Bruce wasn't satisfied to be behind the camera. He wanted his name up in lights. As driven as Bruce was, I had no doubt that he would become a major star.

CHAPTER 10

Humble Spirit; Warrior's Heart

I was scheduled to fight again in the Internationals on August 12, 1967. The previous year I had won the middleweight division but lost the Grand Championship. My goal this time was to win it all.

It was probably going to be the toughest competition I had ever faced. I entered the ring for the first match at 8:00 a.m. and competed until 6:00 p.m. I fought eleven matches and won them all, winning the middleweight division. That same evening I had to fight Carlos Bunda, the lightweight black belt champion. If I beat him, I would then fight the winner of the light-heavyweight and heavyweight divisions for the International Grand Championship.

Joe Lewis had won the heavyweight division, so the odds were good that he and I would meet again for the championship. First, I had to defeat Carlos, which I did, and Joe defeated the light heavyweight, setting up our third fight for the Grand Championship in two years!

Unlike the last two fights I'd had with Joe, this one was more of a chess game. Neither of us wanted to make a wrong move. The match went into overtime with neither of us scoring. The one who scored the first point would be the winner and grand champion.

I attacked Joe, but he defended magnificently. I relaxed for a moment as though I had finished my attack. When I saw him relax, too, I shot forward executing a backhand strike to his face. The judges raised their flags signifying the point was scored. I was the International Grand Champion! As I started in Joe's direction to shake hands with him, my students rushed into the ring, picked me up in the air, and carried me around the ring screaming with jubilation. My brother, Wieland, had competed in the heavyweight division, taking third place. Guess who beat him — Joe Lewis.

Meanwhile Joe's face remained sullen, obviously shocked and dejected at the defeat. He didn't even attempt to congratulate me. Joe had a tough time losing, and he didn't lose very often; when he did, it was a shock to his system. Now he had lost to me three times. Joe went on to a stellar career, always ranked among the top contenders in nearly every tournament in which he competed, but any time I saw him, I recognized that he was still looking for a way to beat me.

It had been an incredible year for me as a competitor. I was undefeated throughout 1967, having won more than thirty tournaments and was rated the number one fighter by *Black Belt* magazine. I planned on retiring from competition to concentrate on my schools. I had become business partners with Bob Wall, a karate champion in his own right, and our schools were doing very well as a result of Bob's expertise and my newfound fame as a karate champion.

My plan to retire changed when Ed Parker, the promoter of the Internationals, told me that if I defended my title the next year and won, I would have my name inscribed on a large silver bowl. That may seem like an insignificant achievement to someone unfamiliar with karate competition. But nobody had ever won the Internationals two years in a row, and I just had to have my name on that silver bowl!

Prior to the 1968 Internationals, I wasn't training as hard as I should have been due to the demands of teaching at my martial arts schools. That was a big mistake. Before the 1968 Internationals, I had agreed to fight in Allan Steen's tournament in Dallas, Texas. I made the finals along with Fred Wren, Skipper Mullins, and Joe Lewis. Fred was to be my first opponent. A top competitor, he was an aggressive fighter, so I knew that I had to be prepared to defend myself. I was right; our match turned into a real brawl.

During the early stages I faked a low kick and then snapped it to Fred's head, but he blocked it. While my foot was still in the air, I saw his punch coming straight at my face. I thought, *Oh, no, I hope he pulls it because there's no way I can stop it.* The next thing I knew I was on my back, and my nose was broken. Jim Harrison, one of the line judges, saw the blood gushing from my nose, so he jumped into the ring, grabbed my nose, and pulled it. I heard the bone crunching. Ouch! The pain seared through my head.

Jim knew what he was doing, however. He straightened my nose out, and we went right on fighting! In Dallas at that time, the judges didn't penalize fighters for making contact, so Fred had scored a point.

I realized that if I was going to win this match, I would have to hit Fred a lot harder. I didn't intend to retaliate, however, and hit him in the face. But I knew if I didn't stop him, he would keep coming after me.

When we squared off again, Fred rushed in. I hit him hard in the stomach, knocking the wind out of him. He had to suck air. Bending over and gasping for breath is the most embarrassing thing in the world for a karate fighter. That gave me a point. I needed one more to win.

We went at it again. I hit Fred harder a second time in the stomach. He dropped to his knees, and the match was over.

My next fight was with Skipper Mullins, whom I defeated, but not without receiving some painful bruises. Then Joe and I fought for the championship. I had never beaten Joe the same way twice, and he was as wary of me as I was of him. Neither of us was able to score in the early stages of the match.

One of Joe's favorite moves was a side kick, which I usually blocked. I decided that the next time I saw the side kick coming, I would drop to the floor and kick up between his legs making light contact in the groin area. Everything worked perfectly. I didn't want to cause him any injury, so I controlled the kick, ending up just short of light contact, but by doing so, I also missed scoring the point.

We stalked each other again when suddenly Joe closed the distance between us with incredible speed and grabbed the sleeve of my *gi*, ripping it right off my arm. He spun me around with my back to him and punched me in the kidneys, scoring a point and winning the match just as the bell rang.

After the match I congratulated Joe on his win. Until that time he and I had never gotten along well because he couldn't handle losing to me. But after beating me that night, he became much friendlier.

When I returned home from Dallas, I was extremely sore from the bruises I'd suffered in the tournament, and my broken nose had begun to ache mercilessly. I fell into bed exhausted. The next morning I awoke with a bad headache. My son, Eric, who was still a toddler, was so excited to see me, he climbed onto the bed and started jumping up and down. I was lying on my back with my eyes shut, when somehow, Eric lost his balance; he fell and landed on top of me. His head crashed smack against my nose, breaking it again! The pain was excruciating as I had to have my nose reset for the second time in two days.

Later that year I went to Silver Spring, Maryland, to compete in a tournament. As usual the competitors lined up and fought whoever was in line next to them. I stepped in line alongside a young man who had just earned his black belt. I was to be his opponent in his first fight. Knowing that I was one of the top-rated fighters in the country, he became so nervous that he got sick to his stomach and had to dash into the bathroom!

When he returned to the tournament area, I tried to set his mind at ease. Before the fight I went over and put my arm around him. "Don't worry," I said. "You'll do just fine."

When we got into the ring, I was feeling sorry for him and mentally planned to ease up on him. The result?

He beat me!

I determined that I would never again make the mistake of being overconfident.

Shortly before the 1968 Internationals, I received a call from Bruce Lee, who told me that he had been signed as a stunt co-ordinator for a film called *The Wrecking Crew*, starring Dean Martin and Elke Sommer.

"There's a small role in it that I think you'd be good for," Bruce said. "You'll play Elke's bodyguard, fight Dean Martin, and have one line of dialogue. Are you interested?"

"I sure am!" I replied.

Although I had no clue as to what acting was about, I figured I'd give it a shot. Bruce told me the date that I was to report on the set. It was the day after the Internationals.

When I stepped into the ring at the Internationals, I was in peak condition. I was looking forward to a rematch with Joe Lewis, but he was disqualified for injuring one of his opponents. Instead I was to fight Skipper Mullins, the number three nationally rated fighter from Texas, for the Grand Championship. Although Skipper had the baby-faced look of a freshly scrubbed teenager, he stood about six feet, three inches tall and was a tough competitor. He was also a good friend who trained occasionally at my studio.

I had beaten Skipper five times in previous tournaments, but Skipper was not a fighter to take lightly. Every match we'd ever had was close. He was rated number three for good reason. In the locker room before the match, I told Skipper, "I have my first part in a movie tomorrow. Beat on my body, but try not to hit me in the face. I don't want to go on the set looking like I've been in a brawl." I probably wouldn't have considered making such a request of another fighter, but because of Skipper's and my friendship, I felt comfortable in asking. I wasn't suggesting that he back off his intensity or throw the fight; I was just asking him to avoid excessive contact to my face.

Skipper smiled. "OK," he said, "but you'll owe me one."

The Grand Championship match was to be three minutes in duration. The fighter with the most points at the end would be the winner.

Skipper and I met in the center of the ring and bowed. Skipper was famous for his kicks and rarely used his hands. I knew that one of his favorite opening moves was a forty-five degree, roundhouse kick, which I anticipated. I blocked it, just as I had in previous fights. But, this time, Skipper followed up with a back fist, a technique he had never used on me before. I never saw his fist coming, and it caught me flush on my left eye. I knew I was going to have a real shiner.

Skipper, who was leading by three points with a little over a minute left, kept running out of the ring trying to run the time out. I knew I had to keep him in the ring somehow, so I growled to him, "Skipper, why don't you stay in the ring and fight like a man?" I saw his face flush. He didn't run out of the ring again, and I hit him with a rapid-fire series of kicks and punches that netted me four quick points and the victory.

Later I told him, "I can't believe you'd let me get to you like that. You should have said, 'We'll talk about it after I'm grand champion.'"

My name was inscribed on the large silver bowl. But I had something besides the bowl to remind me of my victory. The next day I showed up on the film set with a shiner that took a makeup artist an hour to hide!

I was fascinated as I entered the film studio to prepare for my film debut. I had never really been on a film set before, and I wasn't quite sure what to expect. The studio was a large complex, and the room in which we were to be working was a huge cube with extremely high ceilings; enormous bright lights, and wires strewn everywhere. Dozens of people were hustling in every direction like a bunch of worker ants, and I wondered how they possibly made a movie out of all this chaos. Eventually the director took charge, and we got down to work.

Like most people at that time, I was unfamiliar with how films are made. I thought that the moviemakers simply turned the cameras on, and the actors all performed their parts, similar to a high school play. Was I ever wrong! It took hours to work through every scene change. The lights had to be rearranged, the camera angles worked out, and the actors had to be instructed and placed.

My film debut consisted of only one line of dialogue. As Dean Martin entered a nightclub, I was to step in front of him and say, "May I, Mr. Helm?" I was to open the palm of my hand, which meant I wanted him to hand me his gun before he walked into a booth where Elke Sommer and Nigel Greene were sitting. The sequence was to end with a fight between Dean and me.

For the previous two weeks I had gone over and over that one line, saying it into my bathroom mirror, trying to find the perfect way to deliver it. When the cameras started to roll, Dean entered on cue. As he came closer to me, I could feel my throat tightening up and my body getting rigid. My one line came out in a whisper, "May I, Mr. Helm?"

Dean didn't seem to notice my hoarseness and dutifully gave me the pistol. I thought, *There goes my movie career. I couldn't even say one line!* Luckily, the director couldn't have cared less about my line, as long as it led to a fight.

Next we started the fight scene. Dean was to be photographed in the first part of the fight and then to be doubled by Mike Stone, a karate expert. For the opening shot I was supposed to throw a spinning heel kick over Dean's head. I asked him how far he planned to drop so I could calculate how close I could kick over his head. He told me not to worry; he'd drop way down and bend his knees about halfway to the floor.

The director called, "Action," and I sprang into my role perfectly. There was only one problem. Dean forgot to bend his knees! I hit him flush on the shoulder and sent him flying across the set. The director was horrified, but Dean was good-natured about the accident. "I'm OK," he said. "Let's do it again."

When we did the retake, I decided to kick high above Dean's head, just in case he didn't drop down. But this time he sank to a squatting position on the floor. My kick went about four feet over his head. The remainder of the actual fighting was done by Mike Stone. Then Dean came back on the set for the conclusion. The tussle between Dean and me ended with the star of the movie dropping down and kicking me into a table and several chairs. I may have been a grand champion karate expert, but Dean was "Matt Helm"!

Although I hadn't performed up to my own expectations, the scene looked fine on film. I enjoyed being in the movie, but it was not an experience I was in a hurry to repeat. I had been too tense, too unsure of myself; I had never acted before and didn't know what to expect, so I couldn't prepare properly. I was disappointed in my performance, but I wasn't worried about it. After all, I had no illusions about being a film star. Acting was interesting, but I saw myself as a professional martial arts teacher, teaching and opening more schools, with my life revolving around the education of my students. I would probably be teaching martial arts to this day, had my schools not encountered difficulties. I'll tell you more about that later, but for now the acting job did have a residual benefit: it got me into the Screen Actors Guild.

As a result of all the publicity I had gotten from my tournament wins, I received a message from an advertising agency representing Black Belt Cologne. They were looking for a karate expert to do a commercial and wanted to see some film of me breaking something. I thought, *A television commercial could be a big deal. It would give me prestige and exposure, which would help me attract more students.* Also, the money I was to be paid would be welcome.

I videotaped myself breaking burning cinder blocks and some boards. I sent the tape to the agency, and I was signed for the commercial. Bob Wall and Mike Stone, two of the top martial artists in the nation, flew to New York with me to help out.

During the four days of filming the commercial, I broke more than three thousand roofing tiles, and I kicked, punched, and chopped my way through four hundred boards held by Bob and Mike, who were showered by the bits and pieces. By the time the commercial was finished, I was so sick of breaking cinder blocks and boards that I never wanted to see another piece of building material ever again!

My plan to stop competing was delayed further when, late in 1968, fight promoter Aaron Banks called from New York. He asked me to fight for the World Professional Middleweight title against Louis Delgado at the Waldorf-Astoria Hotel in New York City. I had faced Louis in two previous tournaments, winning one and losing one. Louis was a talented and versatile fighter, a few years younger than me. Recalling my hard-fought battles with Delgado, I knew I was going to have another real fight on my hands if I accepted the challenge. Nevertheless, I agreed to the fight.

In the professional ranks competitors fight for three rounds, three minutes each, similar to professional boxing. Early in the first round, Delgado hit me with a spinning heel kick, cracking a bone in my jaw and dropping me to my knees. My adrenaline level was so intense, however, that I hardly noticed the pain and went on with the bout!

I used a judo sweep to take Louis's legs out from under him. He crashed to the mat with arms outstretched to break his fall. As I dropped down to punch him, my knee landed on his arm and cracked a bone in it. Neither of us knew the extent of the damage, however, because we kept fighting until the match was over, and I was declared the winner. We rode to the hospital together. My broken jaw had to be wired shut, and Louis had to have a cast put on his arm. We didn't look much like karate champions as we exited the hospital that night.

Although winning the pro title was satisfying, I realized that the most gratifying part of my martial arts career was working toward my goals. Winning the small tournaments in the early stages of my career had been just as exciting as winning the World Professional Championship. More and more I was coming to realize that the rewarding part of life is the journey, not the destination.

At the height of the Vietnam war, both of my brothers, Wieland and Aaron, enlisted in the US Army. As a veteran myself, I understood their desire to serve, and I concurred with their decision to enlist. Aaron was stationed in Korea, and Wieland was sent to Vietnam. As Wieland headed off to Nam, I hugged and kissed my brother and said, "I'm going to miss you. Be careful."

In 1970, I was refereeing a tournament in California when I heard an announcement over the loudspeaker, "Chuck Norris, you have an urgent call." I hustled over to the phone.

I recognized the muffled voice of my mother-in-law, and she was crying. "What's wrong, Evelyn?" I asked her.

"Your brother, Wieland, has been killed in Vietnam."

If I had been kicked in the stomach by a dozen karate champions at the same time, it could not have impacted me more. I staggered back away from the phone as though that would somehow make Evelyn's words untrue. It didn't.

I hung up the phone, moving in what felt like slow motion. For a long time I couldn't function; I simply sat in shock, thinking about my little brother, Wieland, my best friend whom I would never see again in this life. Right there, in front of anyone who cared to see, I wept uncontrollably.

When Wieland had been twelve years old, he'd once had a premonition that he would not live to be twenty-eight. Wieland died on June 3, 1970, one month before his twenty-eighth birthday. I learned later that Wieland had been killed while leading his squad through dangerous enemy territory. He had spotted an enemy patrol laying a trap and was trying to warn his men when the Vietcong cut him down.

Our youngest brother, Aaron, received an emergency leave from the Army, permitting him to come home from Korea, where he had been stationed. The US government also made arrangements for Wieland's body to be shipped home for the funeral. I tried to help my mom with all the details, supporting her through the horrible shock of knowing that her son was coming home, but she'd never again hear his voice, see his smile, or recognize the sparkle in his eyes that seemed to light up a room. Only someone who has lost a loved one in such a manner can know the pain that our family felt.

Although God has blessed me with a wonderful, large family, I still miss my brother terribly. I think of Wieland often and am comforted only by the certainty that one day I will be giving him a great big hug in heaven.

CHAPTER 11

Material Wins; Emotional Losses

Bob Wall and I had formed a partnership in 1967 to operate my martial arts schools. With me as the chief instructor and with Bob's organizational skills, we soon had three prosperous martial arts schools. By 1970, we were doing so well that a large corporation offered to acquire our business and open hundreds of other Chuck Norris Studios nationwide. Bob and I discussed our options and decided to sell. We figured that 2 percent of hundreds of studios was better than 100 percent of three studios.

Bob and I received $60,000 apiece for our studios and a $3,000-per-month salary. I was to continue running the instructional program, and Bob was to head the sales program. It was the ideal situation. We could still be involved with the students while somebody else handled the business and paid us to do what we loved.

When Dianne and I received our check, one of the first things we did was to purchase a new home in Rolling Hills Estates, a secluded residential area of Los Angeles. I also bought a gold Cadillac. With a regular income and sixty grand in the bank at thirty years of age, I felt flush with cash! There's an old saying, "Easy come, easy go," and I was about to discover exactly what that meant.

Most of us are tempted to think that when things are not going well in our personal relationships, material things will make up for the emotional lacking. But getting more or nicer stuff rarely improves a struggling relationship. I know it didn't for Dianne and me.

By 1972, Dianne and I had already begun to develop divergent interests, and it was becoming increasingly clear that our relationship was in trouble. We argued more frequently, and neither of us was happy with what we saw happening in our marriage. We separated, and Dianne took our boys with her. I was devastated at their departure and plunged into a depression. Nothing I tried filled the void in my life. My family was gone, and God seemed a million miles away. I was lonely and miserable but determined to pick myself up and go on with life.

Four months later Bruce Lee telephoned me one morning. He said that two pictures he had made in Hong Kong were big box-office successes. He wanted me to be in his next film, *Return of the Dragon*, which he was also going to direct. "I want you to be my opponent. We'll have a fight in the Coliseum in Rome," he crowed with excitement. "Two gladiators in a fight to the death! Best of all, we can choreograph it ourselves. I promise you the fight will be the highlight of the film."

"Great," I said. "Who wins?"

"I do," Bruce said with a laugh. "I'm the star!"

"Oh, you're going to beat up on the current world karate champion?"

"No," said Bruce. "I'm going to *kill* the current world karate champ."

I laughed and agreed to do the movie with Bruce.

I had never been to Europe before, so I asked Bob Wall, my good friend and karate school partner, to go with me. When we arrived at Leonardo da Vinci Airport in Rome, Bruce Lee was waiting with a camera crew to photograph us getting off the plane. Bruce wanted to use our arrival footage as an insert for the film. Since Bob had come with me, Bruce decided to use him in the film, too.

It had been two years since I had last seen Bruce, but he was as cordial as ever. He was not embarrassed by male affection, and he gave us each a warm hug before he led us to a waiting car.

For the scene in the Coliseum, Bruce wanted me to look more formidable as his opponent. I weighed about 162 pounds to his 145, and he wanted me to gain at least twenty pounds. Fortunately, I have a very slow metabolism and can put on seven pounds in less than a week if I cut back on my workouts and don't watch my diet. I said, "Hey this is great! I get to go on an eating binge at company expense!"

Bob and I spent two weeks sightseeing like typical tourists. We took daylong walks, visiting such shrines as Saint Peter's Basilica, the Vatican, the Trevi Fountain, and the beautiful gardens at the Villa Borghese.

I found a favorite restaurant where I could load up on pasta and Italian ice cream, the best I had ever tasted. Almost every night we ate at the Tavernia Flavia in Trastevere. I started adding pounds almost immediately, packing on the extra weight right on schedule.

Bruce and I went to the Coliseum to check it out for our big fight scene. It was an eerie feeling standing with him in one of the tunnels leading out into the arena. I was reminded of movies like *Spartacus*, in which Kirk Douglas fought in the arena. And I was humbly awed by the thought of the real fights to the death that once took place regularly in the Coliseum for the entertainment of the Roman populace.

The Coliseum was more impressive and much larger than I had imagined. We sat on a weathered stone seat in the vast arena and talked our scene through. Bruce made notes on camera angles. He planned our scene as though we were two gladiators pitted against each other. Since we were doing our own choreography, he asked me, "What do you want to do?"

I demonstrated the techniques that I thought would be interesting, and he worked out his defenses. Then he attacked me, and I worked out my moves. It took us only one long day to put the fight scene together.

The scene, which came at the climax of the picture, took three days to film. It was difficult and challenging but tremendous fun. Although a novice director, Bruce knew what he wanted and how the camera operator should photograph it. I played the heavy in the picture. Luckily Bruce didn't make me out to be that bad a character. When he killed me at the end of the fight, he placed my uniform and belt over me, very ceremoniously and respectfully. As Bruce had predicted, our fight scene became a classic. To this day you can ask almost any martial arts student their favorite movie fight, and they will recall the fight scene between Bruce Lee and me in *Return of the Dragon.*

Bruce, Bob Wall, and I flew to Hong Kong to film the remainder of our scenes. On the day we arrived there, Bruce arranged for all of us to be guests on the most famous local TV show, *Enjoy Yourself Tonight,* Hong Kong's version of *The Tonight Show* starring Johnny Carson.

I was asked to demonstrate some martial arts. I started by kicking a cigarette out of Bob's mouth, broke some boards, and then Bob and I did some sparring. I hit Bob in the chest with a jump spinning back kick that sent him flying across the room. Everyone gasped, but Bob just got up and shook it off.

When we finished our demonstration,

the host of the show wanted to see the pad Bob was wearing to protect his chest.

"What pad?" Bob asked him, as he opened up his *gi* top. The mark of my foot was on his chest.

The next day, in a local paper, someone challenged me to a fight. Bruce was amused by the story and read it to me.

"What do you think I should do?" I asked Bruce.

"Forget about it," he said. "I am constantly being challenged. It's a no-win situation. All this guy wants is publicity."

Nevertheless, Bob was upset. "I'm not starring in the movie," he said to Bruce. "How about me accepting?"

"Go ahead, if you want to," Bruce said.

Bob went on the same television show the next night. He told the viewing audience, "My instructor, Chuck Norris, has been challenged by a viewer. Now Chuck is a better fighter than I am, so I want you, whoever you are, to fight me first to see if you qualify to face him. Our fight will be held on this show so everyone in Hong Kong can see it because I'm going to beat you to death right here."

The challenger, whoever he was, never showed up, and I was never again challenged in Hong Kong. We completed the movie, and Bob and I went back to our real lives as karate teachers.

I'd pretty much forgotten about the movie until it began showing in theaters everywhere. Indeed, Bruce Lee had discovered a winning formula in films. People were packing in theaters all across the continent to watch the action movie. *Return of the Dragon* had cost only $240,000 to make, and the film ultimately earned more than eighty million dollars worldwide!

When I returned home, Dianne and I decided to reconcile and give our marriage another chance. We worked hard at improving our relationship, and I poured myself into being a better husband and father. I deeply desired to have a better relationship with my sons, Eric and Mike, than I'd had with my father. I made a conscious effort to put my family first in my life. Naturally, I taught them karate, but I also attended all of their Little League games and was along the sidelines at every one of their football games and for every soccer game too.

We were an affectionate family, and even our boys were unashamed to show it. For instance, Mike was a star running back on his high school football team, but after every football game he'd run up into the stands where I was sitting and give me a kiss.

Once as I dropped Eric off at school, I noticed four of his friends standing on the curb. Eric leaned over and gave me a kiss before grabbing his books and hopping out of the car. As I started to pull the car away, I heard one of Eric's buddies taunting him, "Do you still kiss your daddy?"

I turned around to see Eric grab the kid by the collar and lift him off the ground. "Yeah, what of it?" he said.

"Oh, nothing, nothing at all. . . ."

Even today, as grown men, Eric and Mike are still affectionate to me. When we're together, we are quick to hug and kiss each other. We never end a telephone conversation without saying, "I love you."

One afternoon Bob and I went to see *On Any Sunday*, a motorcycle-racing documentary starring Steve McQueen. When the film was over, I told Bob, "That Steve McQueen is one actor I really would like to meet." I admired Steve McQueen immensely. He was my kind of man, a doer. He radiated strength and a strong image. Beyond that, I knew that in his off-screen life, Steve raced cars as well as motorcycles, and that intrigued me.

Bob nodded in agreement, and we let the subject drop. Yeah, right. Meet Steve McQueen. Even though we lived in Los Angeles, home to many film stars, it was rare to actually meet a famous actor in Hollywood.

Maybe someday . . . , I thought.

Soon after I returned home, I received word that my father had been killed in a car accident in Oklahoma. I sent a telegram to Aaron, who was still serving in the army in Korea. He arranged for an emergency leave, and he met me for the funeral in Wilson, Oklahoma. It was only then that we learned that our father had had cancer. Part of his throat and chin had been removed, and a tube had been inserted in his trachea to help him breathe. During the car crash, he had been thrown from his vehicle, and the tube in his throat had been dislodged. Although he survived the smashup, he died on the ground — due to suffocation because no one at the accident site was aware that the tube lying on the ground near my father was necessary for him to breathe.

It was a sad time for Aaron and me. Even though Aaron had been only five years old when Mom left Dad, and it had been years since the last time we had seen him, he was still our father. For the first time in a long while, I couldn't help wondering what an empty life our dad must have known. I determined in my heart and mind that I wanted to be there for my kids.

Following the funeral arrangements, I flew home to California, and Aaron returned to Korea. We both had a lot to think about on the planes that night.

CHAPTER 12

True Friends

I was about to start a class one day when the telephone rang. I picked it up and heard, "Hi, this is Steve McQueen. I'd like to bring my son, Chad, in for some private lessons." I suspected someone was putting me on, although the voice sounded familiar. Nevertheless, I suggested that Steve and his son come by the studio in Sherman Oaks the next day.

I didn't mention the call to anyone in the studio because I wasn't certain whether McQueen would actually show up. At the appointed time, however, I heard a motorcycle roar up the street. One of my black belts who was standing by the window turned to me and shouted, "Steve McQueen just pulled up on a motorcycle!"

Dressed in motorcycle gear, Steve came into the studio, followed by his son, Chad, who looked to be about seven years old and was dressed almost identically to his father. They both carried their motorcycle helmets under their arms.

Steve introduced himself and got directly to the point. Chad had gotten in a fight in school, and Steve wanted him to learn to defend himself. I talked with Chad a bit to determine his willingness to participate in the process. He seemed to be a fine young man, so I agreed to teach him.

Chad was a quick study and easily picked up on some basic karate techniques. Steve came to a few of Chad's lessons and observed. One day Steve told me that he would like to take a few private lessons. Steve, too, took to karate quickly because he had excellent reflexes and natural athletic ability. He was a born fighter, not afraid to mix it up with anybody. Once he made up his mind to do something, he went all out. His biggest problem in training was his lack of flexibility and difficulty with executing high kicks. We worked on those two areas for quite a while, and one day we came up with an idea that we hoped might help.

Steve's wife, actress Ali McGraw, invited Steve and me to join her at her exercise class in Beverly Hills. "We do a lot of stretching," she said.

When we arrived, Shirley Jones and Susan Dey, stars of television's *The Partridge Family*, were already there. Ron Fletcher, the instructor, gave Steve and me a pair of flimsy skintight leotards to wear. One pair was pink and the other blue. I grabbed the blue pair. We went into the locker room to change clothes.

It would be an understatement to say we looked ridiculous in those outfits. Moreover, the tight-fitting leotards left nothing to the imagination. Steve looked in the mirror and said, "I'm not going out there looking like this!"

"Look," I said, "if we just walk out there and act like we've been doing this forever, no one will even notice us."

"OK," Steve said reluctantly. He walked out of the dressing room first, wearing his pink leotard. As soon as he stepped out, I slammed the door behind him and locked it. Steve must have heard the door locking because he returned and began pounding on it, but I refused to let him in. I figured that by the time the girls got tired of looking and laughing at him, they wouldn't pay any attention to me.

A few minutes after I heard the laughter subside, I left the dressing room. Steve was sitting on the floor of the studio, talking to the women. I casually walked over and sat down next to him. I was right. The only one who even looked at me was Steve. But if looks could kill, I'd have been dead!

The class was fun for me because I was already limber, but Steve complained about his stiffness for days and, of course, my tricking him. During the time Steve was taking lessons from me, we got to be pretty good friends. Often we'd sit around after class, just talking candidly. One evening after a workout Steve surprised me by asking, "Chuck, how do you know if someone likes you because you're who you are or because you're a star?"

"I'm not a star like you," I said, "but if I enjoy being with that person, I don't worry about their ulterior motives. If you worry about it, the only person getting depressed is you."

Steve McQueen was probably more open with me than with most people, but the emotional wall that he built to protect himself precluded much personal vulnerability in our relationship. Although we were good friends, we rarely allowed our conversations to go beyond racing, motorcycles, cars, and the martial arts.

We both loved doing special things with our boys, though, and when my sons, Mike and Eric, were only eleven and eight years of age respectively, Steve and I took them to Indian Dunes outside Los Angeles and taught them how to ride motorcycles competitively, with the stipulation that they ride them only on dirt and never on the street. The boys agreed . . . reluctantly. Eric, especially, took to racing motorcycles. As he grew older, his passion for racing took different forms, including off-road motorcycle races, racing cars, trucks, and even racing on the NASCAR western circuit, winning that division in 2002.

I enjoyed my role as a martial arts teacher and assumed that the financial matters were being well cared for by our new owners. Unfortunately, I was wrong; my business affairs were in shambles. While they had expanded the number of schools, the company that bought my schools had no notion of how to operate a personal service business in which decisions have to be made immediately. My partner, Bob Wall, and I tried to tell them what they were doing wrong, but they refused to listen to us. Bob finally got fed up, sold his interest in the schools, and went into the real estate business.

By 1973, the owners of our schools were

in deep financial trouble and had lost more than a million dollars. They sold the schools to another group, which, in turn, sold them to an individual who was more interested in siphoning off the assets than increasing the income. He told me that the schools would be bankrupt within a few months.

Although I had no fiduciary responsibility at that point, I didn't want the schools that carried my name to be associated with a bankruptcy, so I asked the new owner how much was owed. He admitted that he was $140,000 in debt, a staggering sum in 1973. "You take over the debts and you can have the remaining seven schools," he told me.

I made the deal with him, but because of my lack of business acumen, I neglected to include a clause in the contract saying that I would be responsible only for those debts listed in the bill of sale. That was a major mistake.

I sat down with a notepad and tried to devise a plan of action. I figured that if I sold five of the schools for $25,000 each, that would bring in $125,000. I had a little money saved that would make up the difference, so I could still keep two schools and keep the Chuck Norris Karate Schools solvent.

I contacted my black belts, who were running the five schools I hoped to sell, and asked each one whether he wanted to buy the school he was managing. All five jumped at the chance to own a karate school. Each one of the new owners agreed to put down $5,000 and pay me the balance at $500 a month.

I called the creditors and explained the situation. I told them I didn't want to go into Chapter 11 bankruptcy and promised personally to pay them a hundred cents on the dollar if they would give me some time. Most of them were amazed at this offer and were willing to accept the deal. They realized that if the schools declared Chapter 11, I'd be required to pay only ten cents on every dollar owed. I reiterated to the creditors that I didn't want to file bankruptcy, and thankfully, they were willing to work with me. They agreed to let me pay them off by dividing the $2,500 I received each month from my black belts between my creditors.

The black belts made regular payments. Everything went smoothly until I was suddenly hit with an additional $120,000 in bills, including unpaid payroll, state, and federal taxes the previous owner had neglected to tell me about. The IRS said that if I didn't pay a minimum of $12,000 that I owed them, they would close all the schools immediately.

I couldn't afford an attorney, so I went to a business friend of mine, showed him the books, and asked for his advice. "Go into bankruptcy," he said. "You don't have a chance to bail out of this."

I was completely broke, but bankruptcy was not an acceptable option to me. I sold my last two schools and raised $10,000. George, my stepfather, was able to lend me $1,000 which gave me $11,000. But I still needed another $1,000 to make the minimum IRS payment.

When I told Bob Wall about my problem, he said he didn't have any cash, but he did have a $1,000 line of credit on a credit card. He borrowed the money from it and gave it to me. I had no idea how I could repay George and Bob, but I was determined to find a way to pay back every penny.

Meanwhile I had to move out of my office. My friend, Larry Morales, came by to help. He brought a pickup truck and a couple of employees. I mentioned to Larry that I had four desks that I wanted to sell for a hundred dollars each. Larry said he knew someone who might be interested and took the desks away with him. Two hours later he returned with $400.

"Wow! That's great, Larry. Who bought the desks?"

"Oh, just some guy who really needed them," he replied nonchalantly.

A couple of months later, I visited Larry at his machine shop. As I walked around, I looked up at his loft and saw my four desks stored there. I realized that he had bought them himself to help me out, even though he was struggling in his new business and was hard-pressed just to make ends meet.

True friendships are based on gestures such as Bob's and Larry's. They came through when I needed them, and I have never forgotten it. It gives me tremendous pleasure to know that today both of my friends are successful businessmen.

I sold my last two schools, as well as my beautiful new Cadillac, and used the money to pay my creditors. I told the creditors about the unexpected tax problem and asked them for more time. I told them that although it would take a little longer to pay them off, I'd make sure that every cent was paid. They were fine with that.

To meet my personal overhead, I gave seminars and taught private lessons. Although I didn't regard it that way at the time, losing the schools and beginning to teach privately was a pivotal point in my career. I probably would never have done a movie had I not made that shift in direction. But that didn't mean it was easy. Far from it!

I was still broke. I was determined to hold on to our house for as long as possible, but I wasn't making enough money to cover even our basic household expenses. I didn't know how much longer I could last.

Dianne had been incredibly supportive throughout the entire ordeal. Ironically, we depended on each other and worked better as a team more through the tough times than we had during the glory days following the sale of our schools. The problems may have cemented us together in a way prosperity never could have. Indeed, we spent four years fighting to save our karate schools, and they may have been the best years of Dianne's and my marriage.

One night I asked Dianne, "What's the worst thing that can happen? We'd just have to start over again. Is that really so bad? When you look around and see the problems other people face, ours seem minuscule."

Dianne agreed.

Then an amazing thing happened. The producers of *The Tonight Show* called. They wanted some information about one of my private students, Phil Paley, the youngest black belt in America. Phil was a handsome, tow-headed, nine-year-old who was small for his age but exceptionally good at karate. We were invited onto *The Tonight Show*, where we did a demonstration, and after the demonstration Johnny interviewed Phil and me. I've done many talk shows over the years, but Johnny Carson's was the best. He was extremely funny, but he was also knowledgeable about the subject of karate. He asked all the right questions — ones to which I knew the answers — allowing me to come off as the premier karate expert in the country.

Bill Marr, a prominent businessman in Norfolk, Virginia, who owned the Yellow Cab Company there, as well as several other businesses, saw the Carson show. He telephoned me the next day to say that his young son was taking karate from a Korean instructor and that he was coming to California and would like to meet with me. "I may be interested in purchasing a karate school franchise," Mr. Marr told me. I didn't know what that entailed, and since he was just coming out to inquire, I didn't consider it a big deal. But I told him that I'd be glad to meet with him and answer any questions that I could.

When Bill and I met in my office, he asked me why I thought people wanted to study karate. I explained my belief that when a person says he wants to learn karate, he is really saying, "Make me a more secure person." I told Bill, "The positive concepts the student develops make him feel better about himself. I motivate students to work hard physically and mentally. At the same time I try to instill in them a philosophical approach to life that will be of great personal benefit."

Bill was interested in my concepts, but he wanted to check out other schools around the country. He promised to call if he wanted to make a deal. Two months later he called back and said that he preferred my system to the others he had investigated. He wanted to buy a franchise, incorporating my teachers and teaching methods.

After we struck a deal, my brother Aaron and Rick Prieto, both black belts, went to Virginia Beach to open two new Chuck Norris Karate schools. They continued running them for five years, inspiring and motivating their students so well that the schools flourished. Bill Marr's schools became some of the most successful karate schools in the world at that time.

The money I received from Bill helped Dianne and me get out of debt and back on our feet. Although I had lost my schools, in time I was able to pay back the creditors every cent I owed them. It was a long, difficult process, but one that was well worth it, financially, emotionally, and ethically. One day I ran into the businessman who had advised me to go bankrupt. When I told him what I had done, he shook his head and said, "I would have bet a thousand dollars to a doughnut that you could not have done it."

But I had, and now I felt as though a million pounds had been lifted from my shoulders. I was ready for some new challenges.

CHAPTER 13

Hollywood Stars and Other High-profile Students

I began teaching karate to celebrities quite by accident. Dan Blocker, a gentle giant of a man, was a star of *Bonanza,* one of the most popular programs on television in the sixties. Dan played the character Hoss Cartwright. Dan had seen me compete in an All-Star Team Championship in Long Beach in 1970, so he asked me to come to his house and teach karate to his five children, each of them with a name beginning with D, including Dana, Dirk, and David. My class at Dan's house soon expanded to include some neighbors' kids as well.

Dan invited me to lunch with him at Paramount Studios where *Bonanza* was filmed. There he introduced me to Michael Landon, who played Little Joe Cartwright in the series and later went on to develop and star in the television classic *Little House on the Prairie*. Michael asked me to teach him karate along with David Canary, who was also in the series. Michael had been an Olympic-class javelin thrower in his younger years and was still in superb shape, as was David, who was a professional dancer. I enjoyed teaching them, and they were both excellent learners.

Michael invited me to join him on a television show called *Name Droppers*, similar to *What's My Line?* The show consisted of guest celebrities, a panel of nine people, and contestants. The panel was to guess which celebrity was involved with which contestant. I was introduced as either Joanne Worley's driving instructor, Glenn Ford's son-in-law, or Michael Landon's karate instructor.

The celebrities were then asked questions and, by their answers, tried to throw the panel off. Only one panelist picked me as Michael Landon's karate instructor. Most of them thought I was Glenn Ford's son-in-law. I did a few more contestant-type shows and got a call from the producer of the *Dinah Shore Show,* asking me to demonstrate some karate on live television.

Dinah's guest was Lucille Ball, and the producer wanted me to do something that would shock Dinah and Lucy but at the same time be humorous. I worked out a little gag with my wife Dianne, who was to be planted in the audience the day of the show. Dinah and Lucy didn't know that Dianne was my wife.

The plan was for me to do a few karate moves and then pick someone out of the audience to show how easy it is to learn some simple karate techniques. Pointing at Dianne, I asked, "You there, would you please join me on the stage?"

Dianne pretended to be surprised and reluctant, but eventually she made her way out of the audience and onto the stage.

"Let's say a man has just tried to grab you," I said to Dianne. "Here's what I want you to do." I demonstrated a technique, and Dianne acted as though she didn't know what was going on. "OK," I said. "Now let's see if you can do it."

We went through it once slowly. Dianne, who was obviously nervous, stumbled along hesitantly. "OK, now, let's do it for real," I said.

I started to grab Dianne, and she reacted like a whirlwind, blocking my hands, chopping me full power in the neck, punching me with all her might in the stomach, uppercutting me on the chin, and then kicking me hard in the groin! I dropped to the floor. The punches hadn't really hurt me, but that last kick connected! I was in real pain.

Dinah and Lucy were in total shock but no more than I was! The audience roared with laughter, yells of approval, and applause.

When the show was over, I asked Dianne, "Honey, why in the world did you come at me full bore, instead of with light contact as we had rehearsed?"

"Oh, I don't know. I got so nervous, I forgot what I was supposed to do!" she said.

"Well, you almost killed me!" I said.

Bob Barker, host of the television program *Truth or Consequences*, saw Dianne and me on Dinah Shore's show and called to ask if we would do some karate on his show. Dianne was thrilled! Not only was Bob her favorite television personality, but he had gone to school with her father in Mission, South Dakota. We enthusiastically agreed to do a demonstration on Bob's show.

We rehearsed our routine and went on *Truth or Consequences*. The same thing happened again. Dianne came at me with full power, repeating what she had done before, including the punishing kick to the groin.

I asked her later, "Dianne! Why can't you control yourself?"

"I don't know why," she answered demurely, "but when the camera starts to roll, I just lose it. I get nervous and overly excited."

Bob was so pleased with our appearance that he asked me to come back on his show four more times. During the breaks we always talked about the martial arts. One day he asked if I would teach him. "I'd like to stay in good physical shape and learn to defend myself," he explained.

I agreed wholeheartedly and was glad to have another high-profile student.

Bob was trim and strong and took to karate instantly. He became so enthusiastic that he converted his garage into a gymnasium. I soon found that Bob and I had a lot in common. Like me, he had grown up in a small town and married his childhood sweetheart. Despite the fact that he had been a star for many years, he was, and still is, one of the nicest people I have ever met. He is as patient and pleasant in person as he is on his current show, the long-running

The Price Is Right. In his case, what audiences have seen on TV for so many years is his true persona, despite what some of the Hollywood gossip shows purport.

Years later Bob was still able to perform many of the karate moves I taught him. He put his martial arts abilities to good use in the golf farce, *Happy Gilmore*, in which he beat the daylights out of a fellow. Although the movie contains unnecessary profanity and sexual innuendo, I laughed uproariously at Bob's performance.

The manager of the Osmond family contacted me and said that Marie, Donny, Alan, Jay, Merrill, Wayne, and Jimmy wanted to take karate lessons. The Osmonds proved to be one of the most disciplined and athletic families I have ever encountered. The entire family was health oriented, and each member was in excellent condition.

When they weren't on the road, the family studied with me three times a week. After a one-hour private lesson, most students are ready to call it quits, but the Osmonds were just beginning to warm up.

They had been training with me for about a year when they prepared to do a road tour. They wanted to incorporate a karate routine in their stage show, and asked me to choreograph it. The act I worked out had Donny breaking boards and Jay and Alan doing a fight scene set to music.

They had been on the road for about three weeks when I received a telephone call from Alan. "Chuck, I broke Jay's nose in the fight scene!"

"How did it happen?" I asked.

"We were getting so good at it that during each show I kept getting closer and closer with the kicks and punches," Alan explained. "But one kick got too close, and there went Jay's nose." The Osmonds were scheduled to perform two shows that night, so Jay went backstage and stuffed cotton up his nose to stop the bleeding, then went out and finished the first show. He repacked his nose and went on to do an entire second show, as well, before going to the hospital to receive treatment. Maybe that's why Jay's nose is still crooked to this day!

A year later Donny and Marie signed to do a weekly variety show called *The Donny and Marie Show*. Donny asked me to be a guest on the first episode, and I agreed. Donny and I did a karate routine and *kata* (a formal exercise) in unison that led into a choreographed fight scene. That first show was a big success, and *The Donny and Marie Show* quickly became popular with a wide audience, as were all the television specials the Osmonds did over the years.

The family stopped studying karate with me when my own career interrupted their lessons. They refused to train with anyone else.

Priscilla Presley called one day saying she wanted to study karate. I knew that Elvis was one of Ed Parker's black belts in *kenpo* karate, so I asked Priscilla, "Why would you not want to study with Ed?"

"Ed can't teach me because he is Elvis's private trainer, as well as his personal bodyguard," she explained.

That didn't make sense to me, but I wasn't going to argue with Elvis! I happily took Priscilla as a student. Priscilla came to her first lesson wearing a *gi* but looking like she had just stepped out of a women's fashion magazine, nonetheless. She was beautiful even when she perspired! She worked hard and was serious about her training, which usually started with stretching lessons to loosen and warm up the muscles. Then I taught her some basic kicks. Priscilla had studied ballet and was able to execute high kicks with ease, force, and precision.

When we began free-style sparring, I put a boxer's head guard on her. Priscilla took it off. "I won't have one of these on in the street," she said.

"Good point."

Once she even insisted upon going out into the alley behind the studio to work out with high-heeled shoes because, she said, that was what she usually wore, and if she were ever accosted, that's probably what she'd be wearing. She was amazingly practical about her studies in martial arts, and she learned quickly and well; she is definitely not a woman to be trifled with!

By now I had received enough publicity as a karate fighter and teacher to attract some attention in the press, which resulted in more new students, some new friends, and even a new relative! One evening, my assistant told me that my cousin Neal Norris from Houston, Texas, was on the phone.

"I'm at Santa Monica Hospital," Neal said. "I was in town competing in a rodeo, and I got hurt riding a bronc."

"I'm sorry to hear that," I said politely, as I tried in vain to place him in my memory.

"Is there any chance of you coming by to see me?" Neil asked.

I said that I would drop by the hospital after I finished teaching. When I arrived at the hospital, Neal was waiting for me in the lobby. He walked up to me and hugged me. "Hey, Cuz!" he said, with his arm still around me.

Even after seeing Neal, I still couldn't place him, but I have a lot of cousins, and he did look like a Norris, so I asked him what his plans were.

"I'm going to find a cheap hotel room, spend the night, and fly home in the morning."

"Why don't you spend the night at our house, and I'll take you to the airport tomorrow?"

"Are you kidding?"

"Not at all. My wife will be happy to have you stay with us, and you can meet our kids."

We arrived home just as Dianne was putting Mike and Eric to bed. As soon as they learned that their cousin was a real cowboy, the boys asked if they could stay up a little longer. They listened wide-eyed as Neal mesmerized them with stories about his life as a bronco rider.

Dianne finally got the boys to bed and had prepared the guest room for Neal, when Mom called.

"Hey, Mom. Guess what? Cousin Neal is visiting."

"Really?" she asked.

"Yeah, he took a bad spill at the rodeo and needed a place to stay."

"Oh, really? Can I talk to him?"

"Sure, Mom. Here he is." I passed the phone to Neal, and he began talking with Mom. After about two minutes of conversation, Neal handed the phone back to me. We said good-night, and Dianne showed him to our guest bedroom. I picked up the conversation with Mom after Dianne and Neal had gone upstairs.

"I don't know who that man is, but he's not your cousin," Mom said.

"What?"

"You don't have a cousin named Neal," Mom informed me.

When I relayed the news to Dianne, she freaked. "Get him out of the house immediately!" she cried.

"Dianne, it's late," I said. "We can't just throw him out."

"But he's an imposter!"

"I know, I know. But let him spend the night, and I'll drive him to the airport in the morning."

Dianne reluctantly agreed, but she insisted on bringing the boys into our bedroom for the night and locking the door. *Great,* I thought, *now we're prisoners in our own home.*

The next morning, as I drove Neal to the airport, I told him that I knew he wasn't a cousin.

"You're right," he admitted, "but my last name is Norris, and I *feel* like we really are related."

I just rolled my eyes. At the airport Neal told me he was flat broke. I gave him twenty dollars and then pulled away from the curb, never expecting to hear from Neal again.

A few hours later, while I was teaching at the Los Angeles studio, my brother Aaron called from the Santa Monica school. "Cousin Neal is here, and I'm taking him to lunch," he said.

"I don't think you want to do that."

When I told Aaron about my experience with "Cousin Neal," and that Neal Norris wasn't really a relative, he retorted, "Why don't you ever tell me what's going on?" Aaron ran Neal off the premises.

But that wasn't the end of the story. About a week later I began receiving bills from various stores where Neal had charged clothes to me. Soon after I straightened that mess out, John Robertson called from his school in San Diego to tell me that Cousin Neal had dropped by and signed autographs for all the students!

Is this never going to end? I asked myself. Fortunately it did because I never heard from or about Neal again.

(Neal, if you're reading this . . . don't even think about it!)

Besides turning up long lost "relatives," my martial arts reputation resulted in some interesting requests for my expertise. David Glickman, a close friend of mine and one of the top trial attorneys in the country, was asked to defend a man who had come home from work one day and caught his wife in bed with another man. The husband went to a dresser drawer and got out a gun. The lover jumped out of bed. The husband, who knew that the lover was a black belt in karate, shot and killed him.

David planned his defense along the lines that a black belt practitioner's karate skill is considered to be a deadly weapon, and the husband acted in self-defense. David called me, and I agreed to be a professional witness for the defense.

On the day of the trial, I was called to the witness stand for cross-examination by the assistant district attorney.

"Do you expect the court to believe that a black belt in karate would have a chance against a man with a gun?" he asked me.

"It's possible," I said. "It would depend on the distance."

"How about ten feet?" the DA asked.

"If the gun was not already cocked and aimed, I believe it is possible."

The attorney asked me to step down from the witness stand and wait in front of the jury. He walked over to the bailiff and asked him to remove the cartridges from his gun and give it to him. The DA joined me in front of the jury with the empty gun in his hand. He made a show of pacing off ten feet and then faced me, saying, "I'd like you to stop me before I can cock and fire the gun."

Holy cow! I thought. *What have I gotten myself into?* I was wearing a suit with tight-fitting trousers and street shoes, not an ideal outfit for demonstrating karate kicks! I looked at the district attorney standing rather arrogantly at the front of the courtroom. *OK,* I thought. *You asked for it.*

The DA held the gun at his side and instructed the bailiff to tell us when to begin. The bailiff shouted, "Now!"

Before the DA could cock and fire the

gun, I had my foot on his chest. I didn't want to follow through with the kick because I didn't want to hurt him.

The DA was nonplussed. "Let's do it again," he said. "My thumb slipped."

The bailiff gave the word. Once more I had my foot on the DA's chest before he could cock and fire the gun.

Bob Wall and I then broke some boards right there in the courtroom to demonstrate the power of karate kicks.

The defendant was convicted of manslaughter instead of first-degree murder.

In mid-July 1973, Bruce Lee called to tell me he was in Los Angeles for the day and wanted to get together for lunch. He'd been living and working on films in Hong Kong, so I was excited to see him and catch up. Bob Wall and I met Bruce in Chinatown at one of his favorite restaurants.

Bruce seemed to be his usual ebullient self, but in our conversation he revealed the real reason for his being back in LA. He had mysteriously passed out several times while working on a movie in Hong Kong. The doctors there couldn't determine what was causing the problem, so Bruce had scheduled a checkup at a well-known hospital in Los Angeles. "I passed with flying colors," he crowed. "The doctors said that I have the insides of an eighteen-year-old."

I had to admit that Bruce looked great. Slender and strong, at thirty-two years of age he looked to be in perfect physical condition. But I was puzzled. "Well, if you're doing so well, what do the doctors think caused you to pass out?"

Bruce stopped short between bites. "Stress, I guess," he mumbled. "Overworked, overtired. What's new?"

Bruce passed off my inquiry and turned the conversation to the enthusiastic reception his soon-to-be-released movie, *Enter the Dragon*, was receiving. "This is going to be big," Bruce said, "and I've already received offers from several studios for more movie projects. They're offering me blank checks. 'Just fill in the amount and cash them,' they're saying. Can you believe it?"

I could believe it. I'd always believed that Bruce was going to be a superstar. I had no idea that he'd soon become a legend.

Bruce flew back to Hong Kong, and four days later I heard the devastating news that he had fallen over dead. I didn't want to believe that. I had just seen him so vibrantly alive, the picture of health, excitement, and happiness. How could it be?

Rumors regarding the mysterious nature

of Bruce's shocking death flew back and forth across the Pacific faster than the jets that could carry them. Some reports claimed that Bruce had died with marijuana in his system, prompting questions about drug usage. Others suggested that Bruce's well-known experimentation with steroids may have led to his death. More outlandish stories hinted that Bruce may have been murdered, deliberately dealt a mortal blow by a hired killer, an expert in Oriental assassination techniques. Some of the proposed explanations for Bruce's demise seemed plausible; most were ridiculous. Perhaps the rumor mill was simply the world's way of trying to come to grips with the reality that none of us is guaranteed the next five seconds. Life is a gift from God.

At the time the official cause of death presented by the coroners in Hong Kong was "cerebral edema caused by a hypersensitive reaction to a headache-tablet ingredient," similar to the rare but all-too-real reaction that some individuals have to bee stings. American doctors regarded the cause of death as a brain aneurysm.

Bruce was buried in Seattle, and because of his strong affinity with the Chinese community, a funeral service was also conducted in Hong Kong, attended by more than twenty thousand grieving fans. I attended another memorial service held in San Francisco, flying to the service with Bob Wall, Steve McQueen, and James Coburn, who had starred in the film *Our Man Flint*. James was one of Bruce's private karate students, and he delivered a moving eulogy of his teacher.

Following the service, Bob, Steve, James, and I flew back to Los Angeles together, but the trip home was extremely quiet. Each of us seemed immersed in our thoughts, pondering the message to us in Bruce's death. There he was, in prime condition, at the top of his career, and suddenly, it was over. Sure, he had accomplished his goal of becoming the most recognizable martial artist in the world, as well as his goal of becoming a major film star, but so what? Tell that to his wonderful wife and two young children he left behind.

To me Bruce's death was a powerful reminder of the fragility of life. More than that, it was a wake-up call for me. It reminded me that as much as I believed in self-determination and fulfilling my own destiny, I was not the person in charge. God was. More than ever I wanted my life to be about things that mattered not merely for a moment but for eternity.

"God has plans for you," I could hear my mom saying.

CHAPTER 14

Power Under Control

Sometimes knowing when to walk away from something is almost as important as knowing how to get started. At thirty-four years of age, I had held the world karate champion title for six consecutive years. I didn't have the intense desire needed to fight again, so I decided to pour myself into teaching martial arts. Whether my decision was greatly influenced by Bruce Lee's death or simply the desire to go out on top, I can't say for sure, but I officially retired from karate competitions in 1974. I stepped out of the ring as the six-time World Professional Middleweight Champion.

I loved teaching, but I missed the constant challenges I faced in my opponents. Even in the teaching studio, though, I sometimes had to deal with challenging situations off the mat as well as on.

While teaching a class one night, I noticed a husky, powerfully built man enter the school. He looked to be in his mid-twenties. He sat down in a chair and pinned me with his eyes, giving off hostile vibes. I nodded to the man to let him know that I was aware of his presence, but he continued to glare at me. I felt a problem might be in the offing.

I asked one of my black belts to take over the class, walked over to the visitor, stuck out my hand and said, "Hi, my name is Chuck Norris." He shook my hand reluctantly. I sat down next to him and said, "I'm in the middle of a class right now, but if you have any questions, I'll be glad to answer them when I'm finished."

He grunted something, and I went back to take over the class. But his eyes never left me. I was certain he had come in looking for an altercation. When the class was over, I returned to him and casually resumed our conversation.

Although his eyes were still cold and hostile, I kept mine warm and friendly. I believe in making eye contact with people because they can read you. Usually you get what you give, and if your body language is nonthreatening, you can usually avoid a conflict. We talked further, and I could sense his animosity slowly dissipating.

Finally, he said, "You know, you're really a down-to-earth guy, Norris. I thought you were going to be a real jerk. But I'm glad to see you're cool." He reached for my hand, shook it, and left.

Had I gone to him and said, "What's your problem, buddy?" there probably would have been one.

I have always felt that it's just as easy to make a friend as it is to make an enemy. I believe that if I can avoid a potential problem situation, life is a lot better for all concerned. If you pit negative force against negative force, there will always be a collision. Even if you win, you still lose.

Ideally martial arts training should help a person avoid physical altercations and other adverse confrontations. Studies have repeatedly shown that muggers and other social predators study potential victims for signs of weakness, some indication that they can be taken advantage of. Usually this has to do with the way a person carries himself or herself. But someone adept at the martial arts moves and walks with a certain confidence. They seem to exude a physical and psychological attitude of strength, awareness, and preparedness. This attitude has little to do with the size or physical appearance of the person. It is power under control.

Personally, I have never had to use martial arts in a dangerous, life-threatening situation. My friends tell me that part of that can be explained by the look that I get in my eyes when I get angry. I'm not aware of doing anything differently, and I'm not even sure that I could reproduce that look under ordinary circumstances, but I've lived with it long enough now to know that my friends are right. I'm a really easy-going guy most of the time, but when someone pushes me too far and hits that anger button, apparently I get a certain look that says, "You better back off."

I don't feel it, but my friends tell me, "It's a look that you give, a look like you are going to kill."

In the few times in my life when I've been in potentially dangerous situations, that look alone has caused challengers to back off. Apparently they pick up on that look in my eye and decide that they better start working their way out of the confrontation, and I always give them a way out. Consequently I've never had to use my martial arts abilities to hurt someone or to defend myself in an attack.

I think Jesus exhibited a similar power under control. Although Jesus was never a martial artist that I know of (although that scene when he chased the money changers out of the temple comes pretty close!), Jesus exuded a confidence that came from inner strength; he is the ultimate example of power under control. Reading the records of his activities, it's obvious that even when he was being accosted or attacked, he was always in charge. All the way to the crucifixion, he willingly allowed the soldiers to take him to the cross. They didn't take his life; he gave it up. That is power under control.

Ironically Jesus described himself as "gentle and meek"; he was a truly humble person. In our society today many people misconstrue meekness as weakness, humility as a lack of power or strength. Nothing could be further from the truth.

Having a humble and gentle spirit does not mean that a person is weak. It means that a person does not have to put up a fake wall of arrogance or aloofness, trying to give the impression that they are "tough." Many times their veneer of toughness is a façade, a thinly disguised attempt to hide their insecurities and fears of failure.

True humility results from an inner strength and a faith that give you the confidence to display that quality without your self-esteem suffering. A Christian can have a humble spirit yet also have a compelling drive to succeed in his or her endeavors.

My mom is a prime example of a person who combines a strong faith in God with a humble, gentle spirit. Mom never preached at her family or at anyone else that I know. But she modeled true Christianity — in the best of conditions and in the worst of times. She demonstrated her faith on a daily basis. To this day people often go to my mom with their problems because they know she cares. To Mom each troubled person with whom she talks provides her the opportunity to share what God has done in her life. Mom's life is a true example of strength and power under control.

While it was a relief to know that I could relax a bit and no longer had to be constantly preparing for the next big tournament, being unemployed was disconcerting. What was I going to do with the rest of my life?

Over dinner one night Steve McQueen verbalized the tough question, the answer to which led me down an entirely new career path. "What do you plan to do," Steve asked, "now that you have sold off all your karate schools, and you are no longer competing?"

"I'm not really sure, Steve."

"Why don't you try acting?" he asked me.

"You've got to be kidding!" I said. "What makes you think I could be an actor?"

Steve looked at me as though he were looking deep into my heart and mind. "Being an actor is easy," he said. "But being a *successful* actor is another story. It requires a presence on the screen, a presence that I think you have, but only the camera can determine that. The camera either likes you, or it doesn't, but you won't know if you don't try. I strongly suggest you give it a try."

For the next few months, I continued teaching martial arts, but I couldn't get Steve's comment out of my mind. I did a little research and quickly discovered that at that time about sixteen thousand actors in Hollywood were struggling to survive with an average income of $3,000 a year.

When I mentioned that statistic to Steve during another lesson, he grinned. "Remember that philosophy of yours that you always stress to students: set goals, visualize the results of those goals, and then be determined to succeed by overcoming any obstacles in the way. You've been preaching that to me for two years, and now you're saying there's something you can't do?"

"I didn't say I couldn't do it," I told Steve. "I'm just saying the odds are pretty incredible, and, well, . . . stop grinning because I'm going to give it my best shot!"

Steve laughed. "I knew you would."

As I was driving home, I thought about the awesome task I was considering. I was embarking on a new career with absolutely no experience at thirty-four years of age, with a wife and two children to support. Then I remembered the story of the bumblebee. Aerodynamically it is impossible for the bumblebee to fly. The body is too big for the small size of the wings, but apparently no one told the bumblebee that, so he flies! That's pretty much the story of setting goals. Nothing is impossible unless you believe it is. On the other hand, if you believe in God and in yourself, all things are possible!

The next day I checked around for an acting school nearby. I quickly discovered that acting schools are expensive! But as an honorably discharged member of the Air Force, the government would pay for part of my education. In the Yellow Pages, I saw that the famous acting teacher, Estelle Harmon, accepted students on the GI bill, so I enrolled in her classes. It was a full-time school with classes held six to eight hours a day. We studied introduction to voice, reading comprehension, and stage movement, as well as acting.

Most of the other students had studied acting in high school or college or had some other formal training. I was a novice, the oldest student in the class, and I felt like a white belt again, but I was determined to learn as much as I could.

At my first session Estelle asked me to read a scene with an actress in which we played a husband and wife having an argument. I was rigid with fear. After class Estelle took me aside and said, "For an athlete, you're the stiffest person I have ever seen."

"I've never been so scared in my life, Estelle. I had no idea how difficult acting could be!"

One of the keys to successful acting that Estelle taught her students was to evoke powerful emotions from our past, drawing on them to recreate similar emotions in a scene. She encouraged us to practice this principle in our rehearsals.

During one session Estelle made each student get up in front of the class to sing and pantomime a song. As I waited for my turn, I sat petrified trying to think of a song I knew. When it was my turn, I walked to the front of the class and was about to admit that I couldn't recall the lyrics to any songs, when suddenly, I remembered an incident from my past. I began singing "Dear Hearts and Gentle People," the song my mom taught me as a child.

I pretended that I was singing as I was taking off my clothes and stepping into the shower. I have no idea how my voice sounded, but I do remember that when I finished, I felt a great sense of accomplishment. This was my first experience with drawing upon personal experiences to make a scene come alive, and I realized that it actually worked!

As a regular part of class, Estelle required the students to play out scenes, and then the other students would critique their peers. When Estelle asked me to critique my fellow students, I always tried to begin my comments by saying something positive, then offering any suggestions for improvement, followed by a final positive affirmation. I would never tell one of my fellow students that his or her performance was wrong. I felt that although there may be a better way of acting out a scene, there was never a wrong way. I always tried to tell the students what I liked about their performances. Sometimes I'd say, "If it were me, I might have tried it this way," but I'd never condemn a student or say anyone had done a part wrong. Most of the students did something similar with me when I was being critiqued.

One day I played a scene in which I thought I had performed rather well. As usual Estelle chose a student to critique my performance. For some reason the guy tore into me. He shredded everything I had done in the scene, concluding with several caustic remarks. "You're the worst actor I've ever seen. What makes you think you can ever be an actor anyhow?" he railed.

I could feel my blood boiling and rushing to my face as the guy continued to skewer me in front of Estelle and all the other students. I was embarrassed, and I was getting angry. "Who are you to tell me how to act?" I retorted. "You haven't been here any longer than I have. You're not an experienced actor."

I turned to Estelle, and said, "Estelle, I'll

185

take criticism from you because you know what you're talking about. But I'm not going to take it from this guy." I walked out of acting class and never went back although I still recall some of Estelle's acting lessons with great gratitude.

With my limited acting experience, I decided to go out on some auditions for parts in television shows and movies. My first audition was for a bit part in a movie. Imagine my surprise when I walked in to the audition and saw more than forty other fellows waiting to try out for one part! I recognized several of the actors and thought, *What chance do I have against these guys?* Needless to say, I didn't get the part.

As a martial arts teacher, I always tried to set a positive example for my students. Now, as a fledgling actor, in my imagination that was the type of character I hoped to play one day. I am quiet and reserved by nature, but I have strong principles. I wanted to develop a character with similar attitudes and values, a man who used his karate ability to fight against injustice.

Once I had the right mental image, the next question was, how am I going to get the chance to do it? Since the death of Bruce Lee, film producers no longer felt that karate movies would be profitable. I realized that if I waited for a producer to come knocking on my door, I'd be waiting a long time. There was only one thing to do. I would make my own break and come up with my own idea for a film. Looking back, I'm amazed at my audacity. To think that with the thousands of writers, producers, and other creative people competing in Hollywood, I could develop an idea for a film? It was ludicrous!

But ideas are funny little things. They only work if *you* do! So I went to work, trying to bring my ideas to fruition.

Although I had ceased competing on a professional level, I continued to teach private students, keeping in contact with many of my former students, and more importantly, keeping myself in tip-top physical condition. After a workout one night, I mentioned to a few of my black belts that I needed an idea for a karate movie. John Robertson, one of my first black belts, spoke up. He said he had an idea for a story about the Black Tigers, an elite squadron of special commandoes in Vietnam. "We'll call it *Good Guys Wear Black*," he said.

John and I spent a few days writing an outline for a story about the character of

John T. Booker, a Vietnam veteran whose old war buddies are being killed off one by one. Booker's job was to get to the bottom of the mystery. Neither of us had ever written a screenplay, nor did we have the money to hire a writer. We finally convinced Joe Fraley, a friend who was a professional writer, to write the script on speculation, meaning he would be paid only if it sold. Joe wrote a short script from our outline and brought it back to me. I loved it! I honestly thought it could work, so I set about taking the next step — one of the most difficult, I was soon to discover — finding some investors to put up enough money to make the film.

My reputation as a world karate champion opened many doors, but it also caused many doors to slam in my face just as easily. "Karate movies are over," I heard again and again. I met with producer after producer, but they all had preconceptions about me. They thought of me as an athletic star who couldn't do anything but fight. Because I had few acting credentials, I was unable to convince them that I could offer more to a movie than my karate skills. I'd had a lot of experience selling karate lessons to prospective students, but I'd had little experience selling myself as an actor, and what little I'd had was far from impressive. At the end of each meeting, the producers inevitably asked, "Why do you think this movie will make money?"

I'd stammer around, trying to persuade the producers, but I never had an adequate answer to their bottom-line question. I had visualized some but not all of the obstacles that I might face. Although I received one rejection after another, I was not discouraged, but I was disheartened. And I was nearing a desperation point.

Like any other profession there are many good ways of getting started in the film industry — studying theater in college, going to acting school, doing internships with reputable filmmakers, working in the industry and watching for a break — but taking any acting job that comes along can be counterproductive and possibly even dangerous. For me it nearly stalled my career before it got started.

When Lo Wei, a Chinese director, asked me to play a role in a low-budget karate movie called *Yellow-Faced Tiger* that he was making in San Francisco, I said, "Sure, why not?" Lo Wei said the movie would be shown only in Asia. I didn't care; I needed the money. Dan Ivan, a friend of mine, told me he had a role in it as well, so Dan and I drove to San Francisco together.

When we showed up on the set, Lo Wei told me I was to play the Mafia boss of San Francisco and wear a hat and smoke a cigar. I told him I didn't smoke. That didn't matter to him. They bought me a cheap suit and a stogie that was about a foot long. My big scene called for me to fight and get beaten up by the star of the movie. Oh, well! I did the movie, got a little more acting experience, and collected my check.

One night while we were in San Francisco, Dianne and I decided to take the kids out to a movie. While looking at the film listings in the paper, I noticed an ad for a film called *The Student Teachers*. I remembered that a couple of years earlier I had received a call from an independent film company producing a film with that title. They wanted me to bring some of my students to a park in Inglewood, California, where I would conduct a karate class with two of the stars.

The producers told me that the movie was about a couple of teachers who were unhappy with the teaching methods in public schools, so they broke off with the system and created a different learning environment. It all sounded innocent enough, so I brought my two young sons, my brother Aaron, and about twenty other students to Inglewood. We spent a balmy afternoon shooting a scene in which I taught the two stars and my students karate moves on the grass. That was it. I never heard anything else about it. But now the movie was playing in San Francisco.

I suggested to Dianne that we all go see the movie because Mike and Eric might enjoy seeing themselves on the screen, and I, too, was curious as to how the movie had turned out. The theater was in a rundown, tough section of the city. When we arrived, Dianne said, "I'm not going to a movie here."

"Oh, Dianne, don't worry," I said. "Let's just go in and watch our part, and then we'll leave." Dianne reluctantly agreed.

The inside of the theater was worse than the outside. Drab and dreary looking, with worn, tattered, sticky seats, one could easily imagine all sorts of sleaze and evil going on within these walls. Only a handful of people were in the audience when we took our seats. We sat back and waited for the start of the feature. The title credits had barely rolled, when we sat back up straight in our seats. The opening scene of the film was of a naked woman lying on a bed!

Dianne and I covered the boys' eyes. "Let's get out of here," Dianne said.

By then the naked woman was off the screen, so I said, "Let's wait a few minutes longer. It can't get any worse."

But it did! The movie was replete with sex scenes, most of which were a hard "R," and we were constantly hiding the kids' eyes. Finally our scene came on. There I was filling the screen in a gigantic close-up. *Oh no,* I thought, *the one time I don't want to be on screen, and here I am, bigger than life!*

In 1976, I was asked by another small independent production company to star in *Breaker! Breaker!,* a movie about a trucker who uses his citizen's band radio and the help of other truckers to thwart a corrupt judge who controls a town with an unfair speed trap. The title comes from the phrase used by truckers when they called for help on their CB radios.

I thought *Breaker! Breaker!* might be a good breakout role for me as an actor. Equally important, I was to be paid $10,000 for the role, and I needed the money. Dianne and I were just barely meeting our monthly bills with my income from teaching private students and seminars. Although I was the star of the film, the promotional material didn't even mention me, and it never played in Los Angeles. In order to see it, Dianne and I had to fly to San Francisco with my friend, Larry Morales, who was also in the film. There were only two other people in the audience that Monday night. Somehow the lack of response from the public took the excitement out of our movie debut. The first week the film didn't do much business. But when word got out about the great karate fight scenes in the flick, attendance increased. The picture eventually did fairly well at the box office, but because my name was hardly mentioned in the advertising, it did nothing for my acting career.

For three years I knocked on doors all over Hollywood, carrying the script of *Good Guys Wear Black*. One day I told my accountant about the problems I was having getting the script made into a movie. He said he had a client named Alan Bodoh who was a producer and might be interested. He gave me Alan's phone number. I was all set to call, but when I found out that Alan was just a young man in his twenties, I lost my enthusiasm. What could a young kid like that know about raising money and producing films?

Months later, while visiting Larry

Morales in his machine shop, I told him that I was at my wit's end. I had pitched the project to every producer who would see me. Then I remembered Alan Bodoh and told Larry about him. "I'll call him for you," Larry said. He got Alan's secretary on the telephone and told her he had a friend with a script that he wanted her boss to read.

"Send it in," the secretary said.

"No way," countered Larry. "I know how that works. I want your boss to have dinner with my friend, and then he can have the script."

"That won't be possible," the secretary said.

Larry persisted. "Ask your boss if he knows anything about Chuck Norris, the world karate champion."

The secretary buzzed Alan, who had heard of me. He arranged to meet me for dinner that following evening at a Mexican restaurant in Hollywood. Larry, Dianne, and I went to dinner with Alan and his wife. Alan looked even younger than he was, but he was a very down-to-earth fellow. We all hit it off immediately. Alan had already produced two successful, relatively low-budget films including *The Great Smokey Roadblock* with Henry

Fonda, and he had lots of great stories.

When the dinner check came, I picked it up. I looked at the total and gulped hard. I suddenly realized that I didn't have enough cash to pay the bill, and I didn't have a credit card. I motioned to Larry to join me in the restroom. "Larry, I don't have enough money to cover the bill!" I said frantically. "We're trying to impress this guy! We can't stick him with the check. How much money do you have on you?" Larry pulled out his wallet and dumped the contents in my hands. Together we had just enough to cover the bill and even a small tip.

Alan dropped Larry, Dianne, and me off at my home around midnight. We had enjoyed such a great evening with Alan and his wife that I had almost forgotten about the script. I got out of the car and began saying good-bye. "It was a pleasure meeting you," I said.

"Well, thanks, but what about the script?" Alan asked.

"Oh, yeah, yeah, yeah. The script!" I hurried into the house and retrieved a copy of *Good Guys Wear Black* for Alan. I handed it to him. "Read it when you get the chance," I said, "and let me know what you think."

"I will," Alan assured me. "Thanks again for dinner."

Four hours later, in the middle of the night, my telephone rang. It was Alan Bodoh calling. "I've read the script, and I love it!" he said. "I'm going to try to produce it for you. I want to present it to my investors who are businessmen in the South Bay area of Los Angeles." I was so excited I couldn't get back to sleep the rest of the night!

Despite his enthusiasm Alan found it impossible to convince his investors to finance the film. They were mostly local lawyers, doctors, and other professional business types, and none of them had ever heard of me. "No, we can't see gambling a million dollars on someone we don't even know."

Alan called me to say he was sorry.

"Alan, do you think you could get the investors together one more time so I could talk to them?" I asked.

Alan promised he would try to set up a meeting, which he did, following the screening of another movie in which the businessmen had invested large amounts of money.

The night before the meeting, I sat in bed wondering what I would say to the potential investors. I went to sleep with that thought in my mind. A few hours later I woke up with the answer.

The next evening I walked into Alan's office and found about a dozen of his investors waiting. They had just screened their new movie, but I couldn't tell if they were pleased or worried. I started off by presenting a brief synopsis of my story and then told them about my background in karate. When I was certain I had their interest, I pressed in, saying, "I understand your trepidation about putting up the money for this movie. I know you don't know who I am, but there are four million karate practitioners in America who do. I was the undefeated world karate champion for six years. Since I don't fight anymore, the only way my fans can see me perform is on the movie screen. If only half of them come to see the film, that's a six-million dollar gross on a one-million dollar investment. You're going to make a lot of money!"

That's what the investors wanted to hear. They were convinced and agreed to put up the money to finance the production of the film.

A few days later I met with Alan and his partner, Michael Leone, who offered me forty thousand dollars to star in the film. I gulped and said, "That will be fine."

"And if the film does well, we'd probably be interested in doing at least two more movies with you."

"Great!"

When I told Dianne how much they were going to pay me, she said, "You're kidding me!"

"Nope," I said. "We're in the big time!" We were flat broke, but with forty thousand dollars on the way, Dianne and I went out that night and celebrated.

Walker, Texas Ranger

My mom and dad. In his younger years, Dad had a striking resemblance to John Wayne.

Mammy Norris, with my cousin Dean Norris, and Granny Scarberry holding me in her arms.

Mom and I when I was two months old.

Mom, Dad, Wieland, and I in 1953.

Babysitting my brothers while Mom was at work. Wieland, left, and I'm holding Aaron.

200

Serving in Korea with my buddies in 1960.
I'm the one standing on the military vehicle.

Korea service picture,
Air Force, 1958.

Cutting up with my brothers, Wieland and Aaron,
the day before Wieland left for Vietnam in 1970.
Four months later, Wieland was in heaven.

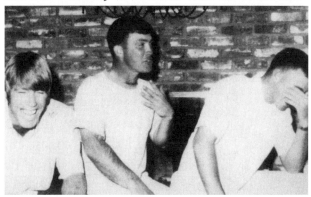

Teaching my first karate class in 1961 at March Air Force Base. Karate was a new martial art in the U.S. at that time.

With Tac Kubota in 1965, after winning my first karate tournament, the All-Star Championships in Los Angeles.

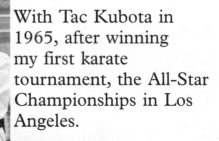

Ed Parker presents me with the International Grand Championship karate trophy in 1967.

Defeating Louis Delgado in the World Middleweight Championships. Louis had already broken my jaw, and as I dropped down to hit him with a punch, my knee broke his arm.

The jump spinning heel kick, one of my classic moves that I used often in movies and later on "Walker, Texas Ranger."

Dean Martin and I on the set of *The Wrecking Crew* (1969), a Matt Helm movie.

Bruce Lee and I at the Rome Coliseum, filming *Return of the Dragon* (1973). The climactic fight scene became a martial arts classic.

After the "death fight." Bruce and I still had blood all over us. We were exhausted but elated that we had gotten the shot.

Kicking Bob Wall on a Hong Kong television show. The host wanted to see the pad on Bob's chest. Bob opened his *gi* and revealed my footprint instead.

Arnold Schwarzenegger and I were friends during our "competitive days." Also pictured to my left is Bob Wall.

Visiting Arnold at "The Arnold Classic," a gathering of body builders and martial artists held in Ohio. Arnold and I have been friends since 1968, long before I had to call him Governor S.

With Steve McQueen after a workout in my karate studio. Pictured are world kickboxing champion Howard Jackson, Pat Johnson, Steve, and myself.

Steve McQueen and I outside my karate school after a workout. We talked about racing, martial arts, and movies, but it was hard for him to open up about other aspects of life.

Just prior to a truck race. I got into racing because of Steve McQueen's influence. Steve said it would be a good escape from making movies.

Filming scenes in *Delta Force 2* (1990). Below, my friend, Howard Jackson, is taking the kick. Howard still handles security for me to this day!

On "Walker, Texas Ranger," the television series that ran from 1993 to 2001, I played a character who personified the code of the west — loyalty, honesty, and integrity.

Preparing to break the world record in a forty-foot Scarab boat.

With President and Mrs. Reagan at Mrs. Reagan's reception for her charity tennis event. I learned to play tennis in ten days time so I could play in the event.

Mike and I jogging with President Bush.

The meeting where *KICKSTART* was born. President Bush, FBI Director, William Webster, Mike and myself. This is a rare photo with me wearing a tie!

At a ***KICK***START demonstration with President Bush. We're now working with more than six thousand kids in public schools every day!

At the top of my game; today through ***KICK***START, I'm fighting for the lives of our kids.

Campaigning for George W. Bush when he was running for Governor of Texas. Senators Phil Gramm, Kay Bailey Hutchison, and Gena.

Being honored by the Make-A-Wish Foundation® in October 2000 with the Chris Greicius Award for Celebrity Wish Granter of the Year. For nineteen years, I have served as one of the Foundation's most ardent celebrity wish granters.

General John Handy, U.S. Air Force, presenting me the 2000 Veteran of the Year Award. I've always been a staunch supporter of the men and women in the U.S. military.

President George W. Bush and First Lady Laura Bush. Little did I know that as this photo was being taken, Gena was in pre-term labor back home.

My mom, stepdad George, and myself. George was an incredible man who had a positive influence on my life.

My older children: Michael, Dina, and Eric.

Gena with her older children, Kelley and Tim.

Asking Gena to marry me. She said, "I haven't said yes yet!" I figured I'd better get down on my knees!

Walking down the aisle after our wedding.

Dancing with Mom at Gena's and my wedding reception. Mom told me again, "God has big plans for you!"

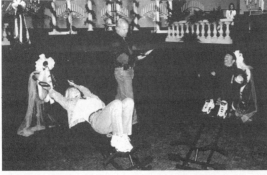

The Total Gyms at Gena's and my wedding rehearsal.

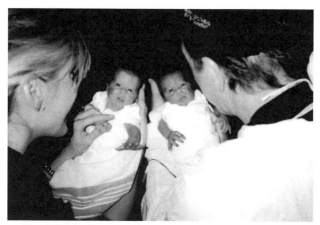

Danilee and Dakota had to breathe and be fed through tubes for several weeks after their birth.

Having fun with the kids at home. I'm thankful to be able to spend this time with our children.

Danilee giving Dakota "kissing lessons."

Gena and I riding the range at Lone Wolf
Ranch near Napisota, Texas.

Relaxing at the ranch
with Gena, my wife
and soul mate.

Today, I'm
enjoying every
moment being a
husband to Gena
and a father to
our children.
(Christmas 2003)

CHAPTER 15

The First Step Is the Toughest

Ted Post, who had directed Clint Eastwood in *Magnum Force*, was signed to direct *Good Guys Wear Black*. He decided that since I wasn't an experienced actor, I should be surrounded by professionals, including James Franciscus, Dana Andrews, Jim Backus, Lloyd Haynes, and Anne Archer. I was excited to have such a great cast, but at the same time I was more than a little intimidated.

Thankfully the producers also hired Jonathan Harris, a voice and drama coach, to help me with my lines. Jonathan had starred in the television series *Lost in Space*. A very proper man, who enunciated every word as though he were reciting Shakespeare, Jonathan worked with me eight hours a day for three weeks. He spent more time teaching me how to speak than he did helping me learn the script dialogue.

One day Jonathan came over to me, put his fingers in my mouth, and stretched it wide open. "Open your mouth, open your mouth!" he screamed.

"Jonathan, you're the only man in the world who could do that to me and get away with it," I said when he finally let go.

"I know," he said with a smile.

Even though I didn't always enunciate the way Jonathan desired, at least I learned all the dialogue in the screenplay, including an eight-page scene that called for me to debate the merits of the Vietnam War with James Franciscus. The shooting schedule called for this scene to take two days of filming. It was a very difficult scene for me because I had to sit through all of it without moving.

I asked Jonathan to talk to the director and make certain that the scene was filmed toward the end of the schedule, so I would have a chance to get comfortable in the role. Jonathan agreed.

When we started shooting, however, the schedule got turned upside down. James Franciscus had signed to do another film and would be with us for only two days. Consequently, the director decided to film my scene with James on the first day of shooting; worse yet, he demanded that the scene be shot in one day instead of two.

I had my lines memorized, but on the night before shooting, I was so nervous that I had trouble getting to sleep. The following morning, when we started filming the scene, I discovered, to my horror, that James had rewritten his lines in the script. I had memorized my speech and the cues that led into it. When he started saying things that weren't in the script, I had a terrible time trying to ad-lib and splice in my replies. Worse, I realized that his character's argument was making sense, and that I was not winning the debate as I was supposed to.

To add to my difficulties, the producers invited a reporter to interview me during the lunch hour. The reporter wrote that I was apprehensive and nervous on the first day of shooting. He was dead right!

We started filming at 7:00 a.m. and finished at 4:00 a.m. the following morning. Twenty hours of straight shooting on my first day before the cameras! I felt as though someone had thrown me into the ocean with chains on my feet and told me to swim ashore. It was a horrendous experience, but I reasoned that if I could survive this first scene, I could survive the film.

Although I was insecure at the start of filming, I knew that negative thinking would be destructive. Negative thoughts bring negative results, just as positive thoughts encourage positive results. I said to myself, *I'm going to do the very best I am capable of doing and not worry about the difference in experience between the others and me.*

When the film was finished, everyone congratulated me on doing a commendable job. When I look back on the picture now, I realize that they were just being kind because I was not a very good actor. But it was the best I could do at the time. The movie was successful despite my lack of experience because I created an image people enjoyed seeing.

It was with a great deal of trepidation that I invited Steve McQueen to attend a screening and give me his reaction. Afterward we had dinner together. "It's not too bad," he said. "But let me give you some advice. You are verbalizing things on the screen that we have already seen. Movies are visual, so don't reiterate something verbally that the audience already knows.

"Next time let the other actors fill in the

plot. When there's something important to say, you be the one to say it. Believe me, audiences will remember what you said. But if you just talk for the sake of talking, they won't remember anything."

He gave me an example of what he meant. In *Bullitt*, he had a scene with Robert Vaughn in which he was to respond with a long speech. Steve read the speech and realized that it was too wordy. He approached the director, who asked him what he would like to say. Steve crossed out the long speech and wrote one line: "You work your side of the street, and I'll work mine."

"Everyone remembered that line," Steve said. "That's what you have to do in your movies. Read your scripts carefully, and if you don't like some of your lines, go over them with the director. Try to convince him to let you say as little as possible, and make your lines memorable." An example of this is Clint Eastwood's "Go ahead, make my day." Everyone remembered that line, a song was written about it, and President Reagan even included it in a speech.

"Put as much of yourself into the character as possible," Steve advised. "We all have multiple aspects to our personalities, and you have to draw on them, the light or humorous side as well as the dark and aggressive side. By using those facets of your personality, your character will become more real to you and the audience. Always remember that the real star is someone the audience identifies with."

Steve's encouragement meant the world to me, and over the years I've tried to follow his acting advice. It works!

Despite their enthusiasm for *Good Guys Wear Black*, the producers had problems finding a distributor since none of the studios had faith in the film's box office potential. In desperation, the producers decided to distribute the film themselves. They borrowed money, rented theaters for a flat fee for a week or so in small towns, and pocketed the box office receipts.

I traveled to the openings of the film, from small town to small town. I did interviews at schools, with the local newspapers, on local television, and with anyone who would talk with me. We started in Texas and traveled throughout Oklahoma, Tennessee, and other parts of Middle America. After a few weeks on the road doing ten or twelve interviews a day, I had learned to recount the plot of the film in anything from thirty seconds to three minutes, depending on how much time I was allowed.

Each night after the show, my brother Aaron and several of our black belt students collected the receipts from the theater owner. Since we had basically rented the venue to show our own movie, the money taken in through ticket sales belonged to us.

Many critics panned the film, saying I should get back to teaching the martial arts because I sure wasn't an actor. Such comments really hurt me because I felt I had done the best I could. I told Steve that I couldn't understand what the movie critics expected. "I'm not trying to win an Academy Award," I said. "I'm just trying to make a film people will enjoy."

Steve laughed. "Look," he said, "the bottom line is that if your movies make money, you will continue to work. If you get the best reviews in the world, but your movie bombs at the box office, you will be unemployed. The only thing you have to worry about is the public. If they like your movies, you'll have a long career."

Steve was right. Despite the critics' sour reviews, *Good Guys Wear Black* did well in the towns where it was shown. So well, in fact, that Alan Bodoh began looking for another screenplay for me. I asked Pat Johnson, another black belt and a close friend who aspired to be a writer, to work on an idea for a script.

"Since you're a world karate champion, let's write a story about a world-class karate fighter," he suggested. The screenplay Pat wrote, entitled *A Force of One*, was about a karate champion named Matt Logan who heads up a squad investigating a gang of drug lords who are taking over a city. The leader of the gang was played by Bill Wallace, my good friend and the world middleweight kickboxing champion.

The climactic fight scene between us was filmed in a sports arena in San Diego. There were hundreds of extras in the arena, including about thirty tough-looking Mexican-Americans. While Bill and I were fighting, they kept throwing things into the ring, causing us to blow scene after scene. No one wanted to say anything to them because they were spoiling for trouble. Of course, we could have called the police, but that might have caused a real hassle.

I suggested to the director that we stop filming while I went and talked with the rowdy bunch. I sat down in the middle of the group and noticed immediately that several of the troublemakers had guns and knives. But a few of them had seen *Return of the Dragon* and were fascinated by the fight scene between Bruce Lee and me in the Coliseum. They had a plethora of questions, and I answered them all while the director looked on, biting his fingernails.

Finally one of the gang members asked me if I wanted them to put on a real rumble for the film. "Thank you," I said, "but that won't be necessary. I would appreciate it, though, if you didn't throw things into the ring." The rowdy guys agreed not to disturb the action again, and we finished the scene without any further incidents.

After *A Force of One* was completed, the producers again had difficulty finding a distribution company. They decided to do exactly what they had done with *Good Guys Wear Black*, basically distributing and promoting the movie ourselves. I started all over again on the same promotional trail, plus some new venues, as well. I had made some friends on my first trek, so it wasn't quite as stressful the second time around, and the critics were a little more responsive to me. But I felt like a Ping-Pong ball getting beaten back and forth. *Good Guys* was still showing in various cities, so I had to fly to one city to promote *A Force of One* and then to another city to promote *Good Guys Wear Black*. I bounced from El Paso, to Detroit, to San Antonio, to Chicago. There were times when I arrived in a city and had to think, *Now which movie am I promoting here?* I stayed on the road nine months with both pictures!

In addition to working the media, I also did martial arts demonstrations in public schools in cities where the movie was playing. That wasn't usually a problem in small-town Middle America, but I wondered if some of the inner-city high schools and middle schools in which I scheduled demos might get a bit more precarious. Would someone in the audience attempt to challenge me?

The demonstrations went off phenomenally well, and the kids in the schools were all polite and receptive. My last demonstration in New York was at an all-girls school, with a student body of more than a thousand young women. I thought to myself, *At least I don't have to worry about any tough guys out there wanting to challenge me.*

I dressed in my white *gi*, did the demonstration on stage, casually mentioned the fact that my movie was playing in the local theater, and concluded my presentation. Everything seemed great. After the performance a large number of teenage girls crowded up around the front of the stage to shake hands with me. As I went down the line, shaking hands, I greeted each young lady. They were laughing and having fun. As I was shaking one young woman's hand, she jerked so hard that I went flying off the stage. I landed on top of the girls and slid down onto the floor as they ripped at my clothes. I felt like a rock star as the school security had to come and help me get out.

I couldn't believe it! The one school that I'd felt safe in, and I'd nearly gotten killed! I sure hope that girl bought a ticket to the movie!

A Force of One grossed more than twenty million dollars, and *Good Guys Wear Black* earned more than eighteen million, far exceeding any predictions. The producers of my films prospered, as did I. My salary increased from $40,000 to $125,000 for *A Force of One*.

When we did *A Force of One*, the producers had a small office with only one secretary. The staff grew to fifty within two years. By the time we made a third film, *The Octagon*, they had a staff of more than a hundred and had become one of the leading independent studios in Hollywood. My three films alone eventually grossed more than a hundred million dollars world-wide! American Cinema went public with working capital of sixty million dollars. I was proud to be a part of their growth.

But then Michael Leone, who was Alan's boss, told him that he did not want to do any more Chuck Norris films, that karate films were dead. Alan argued with Michael about letting me go, as did David Miller, a vice president at American Cinema. David told Michael, "You're making a huge mistake." But Michael's decision stuck, and he fired David. My contract was not renewed, and soon after, Alan Bodah left the company as well.

Ironically, the company followed up with three very large-budget films that bombed at the box office. Soon after that, American Cinema experienced financial difficulties and eventually declared bankruptcy.

My feelings were hurt because I thought that Michael Leone and I were friends, but I would soon learn that in the film business, you're a friend only as long as there's a need for you. Exceptions exist, of course, but not many.

Fortunately, another film company, Avco Embassy, immediately offered me a movie called *An Eye for an Eye*. That film led to *Silent Rage* with Columbia Studios and

Forced Vengeance for MGM. My career shifted into high gear with the successes of *Lone Wolf McQuade*, *Code of Silence*, *Delta Force*, and my three blockbuster *Missing in Action* films.

In 1989, *Delta Force 2* was screened at the Senate theater in Washington, D.C. with about eight hundred people, including many members of Congress and their families, in the audience. Aaron and I were sitting in the front row next to Senators Pete Wilson and Bob Dole. Midway through the screening, Senator Dole whispered to me that he and Pete Wilson wouldn't be able to stay for the entire movie because they had to attend a vote in the Senate. "Fine," I said. "Thanks so much for coming. I really appreciate it."

Toward the end of the film, they got up to leave as did all of the other senators. A few minutes later I turned around in my seat and saw Senators Dole and Wilson near the exit still watching the movie. And that's where they remained until the end of the film.

They were late for the vote, and it was put in the Congressional Record that the vote was delayed seven minutes until Senators Dole and Wilson arrived. Now you know why!

CHAPTER 16

Close Calls

One of the secret dreams that I held close to my heart for many years was the desire to do something in honor of my brother Wieland's death in Vietnam. When film director Lance Hool showed me a screenplay about American prisoners of war in Vietnam, I felt strongly that this was the vehicle through which I could not only honor Wieland but also the more than two thousand other American soldiers who had not been accounted for in that horrific war.

Unfortunately, although Lance and I were passionate about the project, nobody else in Hollywood seemed interested. It was the early 1980s, and our country was still smarting from the embarrassment at the hands of the Ayatollah Khomeini, who had held American citizens hostage in Iran for more than a year. With the inauguration of Ronald Reagan as president and the release of the hostages, the country's mood had improved. Few people wanted to relive seeing American soldiers held captive. At least that was the prevailing opinion in Hollywood.

I went from one production company to another, trying to convince them that doing a movie about MIAs would be both honoring to Vietnam veterans and financially rewarding at the box office. Finally Cannon Films agreed to produce the movie we titled *Missing in Action*, the story of Colonel James Braddock's return to Vietnam to rescue soldiers that politicians and others said had long since been released.

In the climax of the film, my character, James Braddock, barges into a courtroom in Saigon where a hearing is taking place on the subject of American soldiers still trapped in Southeast Asia. The men and women attending the hearing are about to reach the politically correct conclusion that no more Americans are being held captive in Vietnam, when Braddock bursts their bubbles by bringing with him into the hearing room a band of prisoners he has just freed from a Vietcong slave camp.

When the film first opened, I went to see it in a public theater, which I prefer over

Hollywood premiers, because I've always been much more interested in the ticket-buyers' opinions of my movies than the professional critics. One of the biggest thrills of my life came at an opening of *Missing in Action* that I attended in Westwood, California, when the audience literally stood to their feet in a standing ovation following the climactic scene in which Braddock proved that MIAs were still being held against their will in Vietnam.

That ovation validated all the hard work I had put into the film. Indeed, the *Missing in Action* films (we did three) were taxing to make, physically and emotionally. The movies were made in the Philippines on a difficult and hazardous location, and many of the action scenes were extremely dangerous. One scene I vividly recall required me to lead four MIAs into the ocean where we were to be rescued by a helicopter. The plan was for us to be chest deep in the water when the chopper would fly over and drop us a ladder. I was supposed to hold the ladder while the MIAs climbed aboard to safety. Then at the end of the scene, the helicopter was to come under attack and fly off with me still holding onto the ladder, dangling above the water.

The shot was difficult and dangerous, even for a professional stunt double, whom we had planned to replace me on the ladder just before the helicopter flew off over the ocean. When we went to do the shot, however, the wind was whipping too hard, and my brother Aaron, who was the stunt coordinator, feared that the strong winds might blow the stunt double up into the helicopter blades. To prevent an accident, we decided that I'd simply hang onto the ladder a little longer, allow the chopper to pull me out of the water, and then lower me back down.

We began shooting the scene, and everything went as planned. The helicopter hovered perfectly while I held the ladder taut and the MIAs climbed aboard. I was up to my neck in the ocean, with an M-16 rifle across my shoulder. The chopper started to pull me up out of the water as planned, but then, instead of hovering for a moment or two and then lowering me back into the water, the helicopter took off! The next thing I knew, I was three hundred feet in the air, blowing in the wind, hanging onto the ladder for dear life! I felt as though my arms were going to rip right out of my shoulder sockets! When I looked down, I saw the film crew staring up at me, their mouths wide open in horror.

Aaron jumped into a boat and started chasing after us as the helicopter swooped out over the ocean. Meanwhile, the assistant director radioed the pilot, who had no idea that I was still hanging on. He swung the bird around and lowered me onto the beach. The guys on the ground had to pry my fingers off the ladder.

When we all calmed down, I asked Aaron, "If I had let go of the ladder and just fallen into the water when we were flying out over the ocean, do you think the impact would have killed me?"

"Carlos, you were three hundred feet in the air," Aaron said, rolling his eyes. "You'd have been deader than a doornail!"

One of the most emotionally wrenching scenes I've played in my movie career was in *Missing in Action 2: The Beginning.* Braddock is again attempting to save MIAs that supposedly don't exist, when he is captured and tortured himself. When a fellow prisoner is dying of malaria, Braddock finally agrees to sign a phony confession of crimes against the Vietnamese people that his torturer holds over his head, if his captor will give the sick man a shot that could save his life. The torturer dupes Braddock into signing the confession, then instead of helping the MIA, he has him dragged in front of Braddock and burned alive while Braddock is forced to watch.

It was one of the most difficult scenes I've ever done as an actor, and it had to be done on two successive days. The first day we shot the footage of the burning soldier; the second day my reaction to the sadistic act was to be filmed. That meant I had to draw the emotion from within rather than in response to the scene. There was only one way to pull that much emotion out of me. I told the crew, "This is going to be a one-shot deal, so be sure to get it in one take."

When we filmed the shot, I pictured my brother Wieland there in Vietnam, leading his troops, warning his soldiers of a trap, and then being cut down by the Vietcong. Then I saw Wieland in the funeral home, the day we buried him.

We got the emotion on film that we needed, but I was never willing to do it again. It was the best I could do to honor my fallen brother and the thousands of other fallen brothers who died in Vietnam. When *Missing in Action* came out, it earned more than six million dollars at the box office during its first weekend, a phenomenal success at that time. It also received some good reviews, a pleasant change from some of my earlier films. But the best praise of all came from a young woman who told me she had taken her father, a Vietnam vet, to see the film. "It was the first time I've ever seen him cry," she told me.

Shortly after I had done the *Missing in Action* movies, and at the height of Phil Donahue's popularity as a controversial television talk-show host, I received an invitation from the producers of Phil's show to appear on *Donahue*. "We'd like you to come on the show and talk about the Western movies today, as compared to the old Westerns, starring John Wayne, Gary Cooper, Gene Autry, Roy Rogers, and other old-time Western movie stars."

"Hey, that sounds great," I said. "Yeah, I guess I could do that." I thought it was such an intriguing topic, I even took my mom and brother with me to the studio in Chicago, although the producer emphasized to them that, since they were family members, they were to be spectators only. They could stay along the side of the audience but were not permitted to participate in the discussion.

That should have been a clue to me.

The celebrity panel that day included film critic Janet Maslin as well as a psychologist and a comedian, all of whom were extremely liberal in their political persuasions. Phil Donahue opened the show by coming on the set wearing a headband and brandishing a tommy gun. "Is this the kind of movies you want your children to see?" Donahue asked, waving his gun at the audience.

As soon as I saw Phil's outfit, I knew that I'd been had. *Ohhhh, no!* I said to myself. I realized too late that I had walked right into a trap. *I'm in trouble here.*

Sure enough, Donahue started blasting me. "Your violent movies are destroying our kids!" he accused.

"Wait a minute," I protested. "There's a big difference between violence and action. If you noticed, my movies are always a good guy fighting the bad guy; they're stories about good versus evil." I went on, trying to explain what my movies were all about.

Donahue didn't want to hear it. He kept right on verbally lambasting me. Soon Janet Maslin was blasting me, too. Then the psychologist chimed in: "Psychologically, the kids who are going to your films are more likely to become criminals." The comedian jumped in, as well, poking fun at the characters in my movies.

The audience — mostly women — was getting more riled with each passing statement. Donahue was roving through the audience, sticking his microphone under the nose of anyone who looked like they might agree with him. Finally, one young woman stood to her feet, and said, "Personally, I like Chuck's movies. And if you don't like them, don't go see them!"

The other women in the audience soundly booed her. Donahue and the other panel members jumped all over her, as well. She sat down and didn't say another word for the remainder of the hour-long show.

During one of the commercial breaks, Janet Maslin leaned over to me and said, "Chuck, I feel sorry for you."

I looked back and said, "Hey, I feel sorry for myself!"

For the entire hour I was bombarded with incendiary questions, many of which had little to do with my movies or motives and absolutely nothing to do with the careers of John Wayne, Gary Cooper, Gene Autry, or Roy Rogers.

At the conclusion of the program, I confronted Phil Donahue privately. "Phil, to bring me on here under false pretenses was very low handed of you."

Donahue's response revealed much about the television medium and about himself. He looked at me and without apology said, "We'll get great ratings for this show, Chuck. It's controversial, so our ratings will go through the roof."

Sadly, that's the bottom line for many Donahue types in the news media as well as the entertainment industry, even to this day. It's not about truth, right and wrong, or moral issues; it's about ratings and money.

CHAPTER 17

Make a Wish

While preparing to do a new movie, *Invasion USA*, filming in Atlanta, I went to New York to promote *Code of Silence*, my movie that was already in the theaters in 1985. I was staying at the Plaza Hotel in New York, where I found a message in my hotel mailbox from Whoopi Goldberg inviting me to her one-woman play. I didn't really know Whoopi at that time, but since I had a few hours before I was to catch my flight to Atlanta, I went to see the play.

To say that Whoopi's performance was incredible would be an understatement. She was downright astounding, captivating the audience for more than two hours with her hilarious humor and poignant stories. After the performance I went backstage to meet Whoopi. When Whoopi saw me, she ran right up to me and shouted, "Chuck! My man! My main man!"

I looked around, at first thinking that maybe Whoopi had me confused with somebody else. But then she explained. "Do you remember when you were filming the movie *A Force of One* in San Diego?" she asked. "You had a kick-boxing scene in the Coliseum with hundreds of extras in the audience."

"Oh, yes. Of course I remember that," I said, thinking of how it had been necessary to calm down the rowdy bunch of extras in the crowd.

"Well, I was one of the extras," Whoopi said, "and at that time in my life, I was on welfare and trying to raise a child."

"You've come a long way since then, Whoopi," I said. "You are one of the most talented performers I have ever seen!"

Whoopi thanked me and asked what I was working on. I told her that I was preparing to do a movie called *Invasion USA* to be filmed in Atlanta and Miami. "There is a costarring role in the film that might be perfect for you as a struggling journalist who keeps showing up at the locations where I am doing battle with terrorists who are trying to paralyze our country with fear. Would you be interested, and would you have time to play the part?"

"Well, sure, I'd be interested," Whoopi

said, "and I think there's room in my schedule right now." She explained that she was already scheduled to film a new movie, *The Color Purple*, with Steven Spielberg, but if we could do it relatively soon, she might be able to squeeze in a part in *Invasion USA*.

"Great! I'll send the director to New York to meet with you and discuss the role."

When I got back to Atlanta, I told the director about Whoopi and how excited I was at having such a talented actress in our film. He flew to New York to catch her play. When he returned to Atlanta, he told me that he didn't think Whoopi was right for the role. I couldn't believe it and told him he was making a big mistake, but I couldn't get him to change his mind. (If you have seen *Invasion USA*, I believe you will agree with me that Whoopi would have been perfect for the part.) Needless to say, I have never used that director again.

Whoopi's career skyrocketed following her outstanding performance in *The Color Purple*. No longer did people regard her simply as a comedienne; she was an actress extraordinaire!

Invasion USA was a decent success at the

box office, and when the video was sold to MGM, it really took off. The video became the second-highest-selling product in MGM's history at the time, next to *The Sound of Music*. Imagine what the movie could have done with Whoopi as my costar!

I've always had a special place in my heart for children. When country music star Barbara Mandrell and her sisters invited me to Nashville in the mid-1980s to participate in a charity softball game for kids, I couldn't resist. It was a mixed bag of players, including entertainers as diverse as Bob Hope, Roy Acuff, Sheena Easton, Dick Clark, Betty White, Lynda Carter, Morgan Fairchild, Gladys Knight, and Chuck Woolery, along with professional musicians and singers such as The Oak Ridge Boys, Lee Greenwood, Alabama, Tanya Tucker, Reba McEntire, some professional athletes such as Walter Payton and Herschal Walker; and talk-show host Oprah Winfrey.

We had a lot of laughs, played a fun ball game, and raised some money for one of the Mandrell's favorite charities. As I was leaving the ballpark, I heard Oprah's voice calling out my name.

"Chuck! Chuck! Please come here."

Oprah had heard a little boy in the crowd who was crying. When she went over to him to see what was wrong, he told her that he was sad because he'd wanted to meet me, but I was leaving. Oprah brushed away his tears and, with his parents' permission, picked up the little boy, pushed through the crowd, and carried him to where the bus was waiting to take us back to our hotels.

"Chuck, this little boy wants to see you," Oprah called. I stepped back off the bus, and Oprah lifted the little boy into my arms. "There you go," she said to the child. "You get your wish!"

"Hey, there, big fella," I said, as I hoisted him high in the air. "What's your name?"

He was just a face in the crowd, but Oprah had noticed his tears. We were there to raise money for other children, and here was one right in our midst that we had an opportunity to encourage, to say a kind word to, and with whom we could hopefully leave a positive impression. It doesn't take much effort to be kind . . . especially to a child.

One day I received a telephone call from the Make a Wish Foundation, an organization dedicated to helping fulfill the dreams of terminally ill children. They told me that Michael Majia, a five-year-old boy who was suffering from leukemia, idolized me and asked if I would please send him an autographed picture.

"Where does Michael live?" I asked.

"Bellflower, California," I was told.

"Bellflower is only about forty-five minutes from my home. Would it be all right if I called his mother to arrange a visit and personally took it to him?"

"Are you kidding? That would be great!"

I arrived at the Majia apartment with the picture and several items from my movie career. Michael's mother, June, said he was out with his father. While waiting for them to get back, June told me that Michael had had leukemia since he was three years old. Confined to his hospital room, he watched *Lone Wolf McQuade* over and over on a video cassette recorder. "I like you a lot," June said kiddingly, "but I have had to watch that movie over thirty times with Michael. I know every line of dialogue, and it's getting pretty boring!"

I laughed and said, "I have to give you credit. I couldn't watch it that many times."

Michael finally arrived with his father.

Michael was a frail little boy wearing a baseball cap on his head because he was completely bald from his chemotherapy treatments. He stood in the doorway staring at me.

Pointing to me, June asked him, "Do you know who this is?"

Michael nodded his head. He ran over, jumped into my lap, and wrapped his arms around my neck. We talked for almost an hour, mostly about my karate background and how I had started in movies. Then we got on the living room floor, and I taught him some karate moves.

After that visit our friendship flourished. Michael and his parents came to private showings of my movies, and Michael always sat right next to me during the screenings. Sometimes he'd even sit on my lap while we watched the show. While I was in Miami filming *Invasion USA*, I called Michael to wish him a merry Christmas. We talked for a few minutes, and as I was about to hang up, he said, "I love you very much, Mr. Chuck."

"I love you too, Michael."

When I returned home a few months later, I called Michael. June told me that he had died the previous month. Tears welled up in my eyes. "I wish I could have done more for him," I whispered more to myself than to Michael's mom.

"You did everything humanly possible for him," she said. "When he was in the hospital, Michael told me, 'Mom, God wants me in heaven.' He died watching *Lone Wolf McQuade* with your picture in his arms."

After I hung up the phone, I sat there with tears running down my face.

Michael was only seven years old and he hadn't time enough on this earth to experience a lot of things, but the fact that he knew God wanted him in heaven made me sit up and reevaluate the direction I was taking in life.

Besides teaching me about courage, Michael's example also led me to reaffirm my own faith. When my day comes, I want to know that God wants me in heaven.

Since Michael's death I have continued to work with the Make a Wish Foundation, and over the years I invited hundreds of kids to visit the set of *Walker, Texas Ranger.* Each one of those children is special to God and to me, but Michael will always own a piece of my heart.

CHAPTER 18

The Amazing Gracies

In 1987, Bob Wall and I traveled to Rio de Janeiro, Brazil, on a scuba diving trip, so while we were there, we checked out the various forms of martial arts schools. We worked out at several of the schools, and everywhere we went, somebody told us another astounding story about the amazing Gracie family, local *jujitsu* icons. "We don't mess with the Gracies," everyone said. "Those guys are tough!"

Bob and I decided we wanted to meet the Gracie family, so we searched out their school in Rio. There we met Helio Gracie, the father of the clan, a small man in his mid-seventies, who was still a capable martial artist himself. His son, Rikson, was the leader of the younger Gracie sons. Bob and I asked if we could work out with them, and the Gracies gladly obliged.

I had done some *jujitsu* before with Gene

LeBell in the States, and I am a black belt in judo, so I felt quite confident that I could keep up with these boys. But when we got on the mat and began grappling, I quickly discovered that every martial art move I knew was ineffective against the Gracies. It was as though I'd never had a lesson in my life! It was the most humbling experience I'd ever had as a martial artist. Those guys just cleaned my clock!

Helio Gracie came over to the mat and wanted to grapple with me. We wrestled around on the mat, and I was able to get on top of him, when suddenly Mr. Gracie said, "Chuck, punch me."

"Oh, Mr. Gracie, I'm not going to punch you."

"No, no, it's OK. Go ahead and punch me," the elderly gentleman insisted.

"Well . . . OK." I halfheartedly brought my arm up . . . and that was the last thing I remembered! I was out cold.

When I woke up and looked around, I figured out that the little old fellow had put a choke hold on me, robbing me of consciousness in a flash. And my throat felt as though it was going to be sore for days!

Mr. Gracie smiled and said, "Chuck, stay here with me in Rio. Train with my sons and me, and I'll make you one of the best *jujitsu* artists in the world."

"Thank you, Mr. Gracie, but I really have to get back," I said, trying to swallow. I was preparing to do a film back home, so I wasn't able to stay longer in Brazil.

Eventually the Gracies moved to California, where they opened a *jujitsu* studio, along with the Muchado brothers, four top-notch martial artists. Since then, the Gracies and the Muchados have become some of my dearest friends.

Their approach to *jujitsu* is one of the most effective in the world, especially useful for close encounters, which most street fights tend to be. The Gracies could take an attacker down faster than anyone I've ever seen. Even in practice, they could get a person in a submission hold from which it was practically impossible to escape without breaking an arm, leg, or ankle. They also had an uncanny ability to shift from one move to another quickly and smoothly, leaving their opponents wondering what had happened! Their secret was all leverage, not physical strength, but believe me, they truly are the amazing Gracies.

Since 1978, I have headed up an organization of black belt martial artists known as the United Fighting Arts Federation. Each year in July, I invite all my black belt students to join me at a convention in Las Vegas, where we train together for several days. For ten straight years beginning in 1993, the Gracies and the Muchado brothers have presented seminars at the convention.

Once my black belt students become proficient in *chun kuk do* (the universal way), I want them to become adept in *jujitsu* as well. And there's nobody in the world better at *jujitsu* than the Gracies and Muchados.

During the 1999 convention, Carlos Muchado, the elder brother of the family, asked me, "Chuck, why don't you help me out with my beginners."

"OK, Carlos. It will be fun."

Carlos was teaching a class comprised of twenty-two of our new black belts. Young, agile, and strong, these were the cream of our new crop of martial artists, and I was delighted to spend some time with them.

Carlos asked me to participate in demonstrating to the class some holds and how to get out of them. I was showing one of the black belt students how to escape a hold, when suddenly he started grappling with me, trying to wrestle me to the ground.

This wasn't exactly what I had in mind.

But we were already into it, so I maneuvered him into an arm bar, a painful hold that he didn't want to endure for long. Almost immediately, he tapped the mat, which means "I give up!"

Another student saw us grappling and called out, "Mr. Norris, can I grapple with you?"

"Oh, ah . . . , oh, OK." That student and I grappled for a few minutes before I got him in a hold, forcing him to tap out.

Soon another black belt wanted to grapple. I started going through the entire class, one at a time. Many of the young black belts were college wrestlers in their early twenties! I thought, *Oh, man, what have I gotten myself into?*

Victor Matera, an enthusiastic young black belt was in the group, standing by, closely observing the matches. Each time I made someone tap out, Victor would go over to Carlos Muchado and ask, "What would you do to defend against that?"

Carlos would then show Victor how to avoid getting into that particular hold. As I continued to grapple with the row of students, Carlos continued dispensing information to Victor on how to counteract each of my holds or how to defeat my moves. With each student my available repertoire of surprise moves was being diminished!

Finally I had subdued every student but Victor, who then came over and asked, "Mr. Norris, can I grapple with you?"

"Oh, I don't know," I said. "I'm pretty tired."

"Oh, please, Mr. Norris, let me be the last one."

"Well, all right."

We began grappling, and as I would attempt a submission hold, Victor managed to avoid it. He had the advantage of seeing all my moves, plus the benefit of Carlos's suggestions to counteract and escape my holds. Nevertheless, within about two minutes, I had the young man tapping out, as well.

I was nearly exhausted, but the demonstration really increased my reputation with that bunch of black belts. "Mr. Norris made twenty-two black belts submit back-to-back!" I heard one of them say. I smiled, knowing that I wouldn't need any more ego strokes for quite a while.

I love working out with my former students — or the students of my former students

— but it gets tougher to keep up with them every year. On another occasion at the convention, the students were practice-kicking a dummy that was electronically wired to determine the force with which the students were kicking in pounds per square inch. Most of the students were kicking the dummy somewhere in the range of two hundred pounds per square inch. A few of them struck the dummy with almost three hundred pounds per square inch of force as registered by the meter. That's quite a wallop, and I was extremely impressed.

"Mr. Norris, why don't you give it a try? Let's see you kick it," one of my black belt students suggested.

I hemmed and hawed a bit. "Oh, I don't think so . . ."

"Oh, please, Mr. Norris. Let's see you do it!"

I finally acquiesced and said, "Well, OK; I'll give it a try."

I leaped up and kicked the dummy. I don't know what I did differently from our students; I must have hit the dummy perfectly or something because the meter registered an impact of six hundred pounds per square inch!

"Holy mackerel!" one of the black belts

shouted. "Nobody has ever done that. Nobody has gotten the meter above three hundred pounds, and Mr. Norris more than doubled that!"

Believe me, I was as amazed as my black belts! The students looked at me in awe and went back to trying to better their readings. None of them kicked the dummy with half the force my kick had registered.

I'm sure that my amazing kick must have been due to some sort of aberration in the meter, but as far as my students were concerned, I was an Adonis!

CHAPTER 19

An Unexpected Advocate

As a martial arts instructor for fifteen years, I taught thousands of young boys and girls, many of whom harbored deep insecurities that caused a lack of self-esteem. I loved teaching them because as they became more proficient in the martial arts, they developed a more positive attitude and were more secure in themselves. But these were students whose parents could afford to bring them to my martial arts school and pay for lessons.

I often thought about the millions of young kids whose parents could not afford to send them to a martial arts school or some other program where they could receive these incredible benefits. How could I help those kids? That question stayed in the back of my mind for many years, but I was too busy with my film career to pursue the answer.

It's amazing how thoughts we plant in our minds can eventually materialize into actions. My desire to help underprivileged kids didn't disappear with time but instead grew stronger, yet I was as surprised as anyone to discover how God would cause those seeds to grow and who would come into my life to help them take root and bear fruit.

In 1988, I got a call from Lee Atwater, campaign manager for (then) presidential candidate, George Herbert Walker Bush. Lee asked me if I would emcee a political rally in Riverside, California, for Mr. Bush. I was reluctant to accept, partly because I had never done anything like that. Nevertheless, I told Lee, "If Mr. Bush wants me to emcee the program, I'll be glad to give it a try."

I'd been politically involved for some time and had gotten to know Ronald and Nancy Reagan through an invitation to participate in a charity tennis event for Mrs. Reagan's "Just Say No" antidrug campaign. My first brush with the Reagans came about when my secretary called me in my car one day and said, "Mrs. Reagan would like you to play in a charity tennis tournament ten days from now in Washington. Would you like to go?"

"Oh, yes. Tell her I'll be glad to play," I said. When I hung up the phone, it suddenly occurred to me, *I don't know how to play tennis!* I'd never picked up a tennis racket in my life! But I had ten days to learn. I hired a tennis instructor and worked like mad trying to learn the game. Ten days later I was in Washington playing in Mrs. Reagan's charity tennis tournament. I didn't do too badly although I sent a few shots sailing over the fence and into the street! Mrs. Reagan didn't seem to mind, so I didn't, either!

Although some critics have not always been enthusiastic about the pro-America stance I've taken in my movies and in my personal life, I've always been grateful for our country. I'm big on voter awareness, exercising our right to vote, and voicing our opinions. As my mom always said, "If you don't vote, you have no right to complain. You're getting what you asked for."

I remained politically involved throughout the Reagan-Bush terms of office but usually from a distance — until that call came from Lee Atwater in 1988 inviting me to participate at Riverside.

The Riverside rally for George Herbert

Walker Bush was a huge success with about fifteen thousand people attending. It was great fun, and I was honored to speak in support of Vice President Bush. When Mr. Bush took the microphone, he quipped, "I can't begin to tell you how safe I feel standing here next to Chuck Norris!"

The crowd loved it. It was obvious that Mr. Bush and I had a rapport right from the start. I genuinely believed in him as a candidate and as a person of the utmost integrity. I would have voted for him even if I had not been involved with his campaign.

The Riverside rally was such a huge success, Lee asked me if I had the time to go on the campaign trail and emcee other rallies. I liked George Bush, and I was in between shooting and promoting my movies, so I was glad to oblige.

We traveled throughout Northern California on a tour bus, going from one town to the next. Mr. Bush had been tagged with a "nice guy" image by the media earlier in his campaign, but once I started traveling with him, the press changed its tune. "Here come the two tough guys," they'd say. Mr. Bush loved it!

During the campaign Lee Atwater and I became good friends. Lee was a brilliant young man who had a photographic memory and loved watching movies. He had seen every one of mine, and he'd often quiz me about my own films. "Remember when you said so-and-so in that scene in one of your old movies?"

"No, Lee," I'd respond. "I don't remember. That movie was long ago." Later, when I had a chance to watch the old movie, I'd discover that, sure enough, Lee had remembered correctly and quoted the lines verbatim.

I also got to know Mr. Bush during that presidential campaign, and found him to be a very special person. When I first started traveling with him on the campaign, I was fairly shy, which is my nature, but Mr. Bush immediately made me feel as though I had known him for years.

I soon discovered that Mr. Bush is also incredibly loyal to his friends. He doesn't forget those who sacrificed their time, money, or effort on his behalf.

When Mr. Bush was elected President, I was invited to the inauguration, and at the gala celebration I was asked to give a speech along with Arnold Schwarzenegger. I was seated next to Arnold and was slated to speak first. Arnold kept nudging me, saying under his breath, "You're going to blow it, Chuck. You're going to forget what you planned to say. You're going to flub your speech." Arnold is infamous among his friends for doing things like that, but I kept telling him, "Keep quiet, Arnold! I have to concentrate." Fortunately, my speech went quite well, and I later got a chance to sit back and heckle Arnold.

Arnold and I go back a long way. We've known each other since 1968, before he became an internationally known film star. When Arnold first moved to California, he was known as a world-class bodybuilder. Arnold and I used to work out together occasionally. In between exercising, we often talked about our ambitions. I said, "I'm satisfied teaching the martial arts."

"Not me," Arnold responded. "Bodybuilding is just a stepping-stone to me. I plan on becoming a real estate mogul, and from there, I plan to get into the movies."

I had to smile as I said to myself, *How's he going to be an actor when he can hardly speak English?*

I wasn't the only one who had such misgivings. When Arnold announced that he wanted to become an actor, he was turned down on three counts. First, he was told his body was too big and muscular. (How would you like to have been the person who had to tell Arnold that?) Second, he had a strong foreign accent and often spoke in broken or poor English. Third, his advisors suggested that he change his name.

Arnold was undaunted. He set about the task of trimming down his body by adjusting his eating and exercising program. At the same time he studied the English language and struggled to improve his enunciation. Arnold stood his ground, however, when it came to changing his name. Instead, he vowed to make Schwarzenegger a household name.

I don't know anyone any more determined than Arnold. Today we refer to my friend as Governor Schwarzenegger!

Lee Atwater had arranged the details of the inauguration gala, complete with a rhythm and blues band to celebrate the successful election of George Herbert Walker Bush. Lee, who played the guitar in his spare time, got President Bush up on the stage and gave the president his guitar to play. President Bush was good-natured and pretended he was part of the band. It was hilariously funny, and the entire time I watched the spectacle, I was thinking, *I can't believe Lee has the President of the*

United States pretending to be a rhythm and blues star!

After the election Lee invited me to the White House and escorted me on a tour. We went to the office where John Sununu, the chief of staff, was in a meeting. Lee walked right into the meeting, and said, "John, I want you to meet Chuck Norris." John got up from the table, walked over, and shook my hand. Lee then told me he wanted me to meet Jim Baker, the secretary of state.

I said, "Lee, are you sure we should disturb him?"

"Oh, yeah," Lee said, "he's a great guy." Lee Atwater wasn't intimidated by anyone!

I was invited to the White House on several occasions for state dinners to welcome leaders from other nations. I took my son, Mike, to a state dinner for the president of Poland. While President Bush waited on the platform to welcome his arriving guest, Mike and I were in a crowd of thousands watching. A Secret Service agent approached me in the crowd. He pulled me aside and spoke clandestinely, "Mr. Norris?"

"Yes, I'm Chuck. What can I do for you?"

"The President wants to know if you and

your son would like to go jogging with him after the ceremonies."

My first thought was, *Can I keep up with him?* President Bush was in excellent physical condition and ran nearly every day. I was in good shape, but running was only a small part of my workout regimen. Nevertheless, I didn't want to miss out on this opportunity.

I said, "Of course! We'd be glad to."

Following the official welcoming ceremonies, the agent ushered us into a room in the White House where Mike and I could change clothes. A short time later President Bush came in and joined us, stripping down and changing into his running clothes, just like one of the guys in a high school locker room.

Mike and I ran several miles with President Bush, surrounded by several Secret Service agents who ran in front of us and behind us. One of the agents carried an Uzzi hidden in a briefcase as he ran with us. It was a weird feeling but an unforgettable experience.

That evening Mike and I attended a state dinner with hundreds of other invited guests. After dinner everyone was standing around in the ballroom that leads up to the First Family's private quarters. The President and First Lady were mingling with their guests when I saw them walking up the stairs to retire for the evening. I was tired, too, and decided to leave. I was headed for the exit when I heard someone yell, "Chuck!" I turned around and saw that it was President Bush who had called out my name. He was standing on the staircase next to Barbara, waving good-bye to me.

I thought, *Who am I that the President of the United States would call out my name?*

I recalled the story of Zacchaeus, that little guy Jesus saw perched in a tree so he could see above the crowd. Jesus said, "Zacchaeus, come down. I'm going to your house today." My guess is that Zacchaeus never got over that sense of wonder, when he realized, "He knows my name!"

On a much more down-to-earth level, that's something of what I felt when George Bush waved good-bye to me from the White House staircase. What a man! With the weight of the world on his shoulders, he never forgets how to make individuals feel special. I feel blessed to know George Herbert Walker Bush, not only as the President, but as a good man, and as a man I respect as a wonderful husband and father. Whether or not you agree with his politics or his decisions as President, he is a man of integrity; he is the complete package.

The next day Mike and I had lunch with the President and FBI Director William Webster. During lunch President Bush asked me what my future plans were outside the entertainment field. I told him I would like to work with the youth in America, teaching them the martial arts.

"You've done that," he said.

"I know, but I would like to teach children whose parents can't afford to send them to a commercial school."

"How would you do that?" the President asked me.

I told him I would like to hire black belt instructors to teach in the public school systems, specifically in the middle schools — sixth, seventh, and eighth grades — because those are the ages when many kids begin to drift into gang activity, drugs, and violence.

"Why do you feel martial arts can help in these areas?" the President asked.

"I've always believed that a child who develops a strong sense of self-worth will have the inner strength to resist peer pressure, including drug and alcohol abuse, as well as involvement in gangs," I said.

"Martial arts training raises self-esteem and instills the type of discipline and respect that so many kids are lacking nowadays. In other words, it builds strong, positive character and will help our youth resist drug-related peer pressure that is certainly a major concern for our country." I stopped abruptly, suddenly realizing that I was practically preaching to the President! I needn't have worried, though.

The President listened carefully and then asked me how I would implement such a program in the public schools. I said that I felt martial arts classes could be offered as an elective, as an alternative to regular physical education classes. "If we taught thirty kids in each class, with five classes a day, we could teach one-hundred-fifty kids a day in each school. In my opinion the program would have some positive results with these kids," I suggested to President Bush.

Although the idea for such a program had been in the back of my mind for over twenty years, I was literally developing it more clearly as I described the possibilities to the President of the United States.

"That's a great idea!" he said.

Just then Mrs. Bush walked in. "What's a great idea?" she asked.

I repeated the whole story, but this time I was getting an even better picture of what I wanted to do. The entire "Kick Drugs Out of America" program began to take shape as we talked.

President Bush said, "Let's get this program going. What city do you want to start with?"

"I don't know. I really haven't thought about it."

"How about Houston?"

"That sounds fine to me," I said, "but are you sure the school system will go for it?"

"I think I can convince them," President Bush said with a smile. "But you'll need someone to help you run the program. I'd like to recommend Lloyd Hatcher."

"What does he do?" I asked.

President Bush chuckled and said, "First, it isn't a he; Lloyd is a female. She's a close friend of my son Marvin and my daughter-in-law Margaret. Also she's a graduate of the University of North Carolina and extremely bright."

The President also recommended Brad O'Leary, a well-known lobbyist and businessman in Washington, D.C. to help me. Kick Drugs Out of America, the martial arts program in public schools, was founded with Lloyd Hatcher, Brad O'Leary, my manager Myron Emery, and me. We estimated it would cost about $50,000 to fund a school martial arts program for a year, which would pay for the instructor, uniforms and belts for the students, plus a salary for Lloyd, and other basic business expenses. My job was to raise the money to start the program.

I contacted various business leaders in Houston, but no one would come on board to finance the program or even part of it. Frustrated, I told Lloyd I'd just pay for it myself.

"That will be fine for one school," Lloyd said, "but our goal is not to have just one but hundreds of schools. Do you intend to pay for them all?"

I said, "I get your point."

Soon after that conversation I attended a charity event in Houston and met Jim McIngvale, owner of Gallery Furniture, one of the most successful furniture businesses in Texas. I had just started pitching my Foundation plans to him when his wife Linda joined us. I told the McIngvales what I wanted to do and said I was looking for people to get financially involved. Mac and Linda listened to my plans and agreed to meet with me to discuss them further the following day.

At that meeting I told the McIngvales more about the program. Linda took a checkbook out of her purse and started to write out a check. I was thinking, *How much is she going to donate? Maybe $5,000.* My jaw dropped when I saw the check was for $50,000, enough to pay for an entire year at a middle school. With the McIngvale's contribution, the Kick Drugs Out of America program was officially underway in 1990.

Thanks to Mac and Linda's continuing support, we were able to find other people to come on board. Mac, who is an incredible public speaker, began to talk up the power of our program, and word about KDOA soon started getting out in Houston.

The Houston Independent School District agreed to a trial run for one year at the M. C. Williams Middle School. I hired Roy White, one of my black belts, to teach there. I knew it was going to be a real challenge for Roy, because M. C. Williams had a reputation of being a tough, inner-city school.

Our program is designed to help all children believe that they can lead productive lives and that they *can* achieve their goals and dreams. The choice is theirs. We teach our students, "If you believe you can, you will. If you believe you cannot, you will not."

Two weeks after we started the program, I was in Los Angeles preparing to leave for Israel to make a film, when I got a telephone call from Roy. "I've never worked with such undisciplined children in my life!" he said. "These kids have called me every name in the book, and none of them are nice. I don't know if this is going to work."

I thought for a few seconds, then said, "Can you hang in there until I get back from Israel?"

"How long will that be?" Roy asked.

"Four months."

After a long pause, Roy said, "Well, I'll try."

"Good," I said, "as soon as I get back, I'll come to Houston, and we'll evaluate the program."

Roy laughed. "OK, I'll look forward to seeing you . . . if I'm still alive."

When I returned home from Israel, I flew directly to Houston and went to the M. C. Williams School. The principal greeted me and escorted me through the school to the gym where he said the students were waiting. As we were walking to the gym, some kids in the classrooms saw me, ran to the windows, and starting yelling my name and waving. As I was waving back, one of the kids shouted at the principal, "My dad's going to kill you!"

Whoa, I thought. *And this is only a middle school.*

When we got to the gym, I was shocked! I saw about one-hundred-fifty kids in karate uniforms, standing at attention. As I walked in, they shouted in unison, "Mr. Norris, it's a pleasure to have you here, sir." I went by and shook hands with each of the students who introduced themselves to me. We had a question and answer period, and then they presented a martial arts demonstration.

As they were leaving, I asked Roy, "What happened? Four months ago you were ready to give up."

"It wasn't easy," he said. "I just kept chipping away at their negative attitudes with positive affirmations every day, and slowly they started responding. The turning point came when I was teaching class, and one of the students who happens to be the toughest kid in school, an eighth grader who weighed one hundred eighty pounds, asked to spar with me."

Roy said, "I told him, 'A student never challenges an instructor. That is disrespectful.' When the class ended, I had all the students leave, and told him to stay. 'Do you still want to spar?' I asked him.

" 'Yeah, I do,' he said.

"I sparred with him, and tapped him around the face with kicks and showed him that I was in total control of the situation.

"Then he said, 'Actually I'm a better wrestler.'

" 'Oh, so now you want to wrestle?' I got him in choke holds and arm bars. After it was over, he said, 'Thank you, Mr. White. Thank you very much, *Sir!*'

"He left, and told all the kids, 'Don't mess with Mr. White.' The toughest kid in school became my strongest advocate, and suddenly things started falling into place."

By the end of that first year, M. C. Williams was totally sold on the program. Within a couple of years, it became apparent from independent evaluations that the impact of KDOA was much more than helping youngsters resist drugs. Their grades improved, and there were fewer disciplinary problems with our youngsters.

As we raised more money, we began developing and expanding the program to other middle schools in Houston. By our fifth year we were in eight schools and were teaching twelve hundred kids. In our eighth year we expanded the program to Dallas. By our tenth year we were teaching thirty-nine hundred youngsters in twenty-six schools. Our program now enrolls more than six thousand youngsters every year, and the number is growing! Six thousand kids may not seem like a lot to some people, but each of those kids has a sphere of influence. Besides, it only takes one person to change the world, either positively or negatively.

Today our foundation has been recognized as a character-building, life-skills program with the fundamental purpose of giving a young person the tools to strengthen his or her self-image. We recently realized that our original name, Kick Drugs Out of America, implies too narrow a focus for all that we were accomplishing. We decided on a name that more accurately describes our mission: **KICK**START — building strong moral character in our youth through the martial arts.

It's still my job to raise the money to keep the program going and expanding. When I am trying to get individuals or corporations to become sponsors of **KICK**START, I am often asked if our program really works.

I reply that thousands of kids have graduated from the program, and many of them are now enrolled in college, and some have already earned their degrees. Six students who started with us in the sixth grade have returned after graduating from college and are now instructors in the program.

One of the many success stories to emerge from the program is that of Gerardo Esparza. Gerardo joined KDOA shortly after its inception. Gerardo used the principles and discipline of the program to motivate himself toward academic success, a journey he recently completed with his graduation from the Massachusetts Institute of Technology (MIT) with a degree in finance and economics.

Angeline Beltran is another of our successful graduates. After three years in the program, Angeline became the first person in her family to graduate from high school. She graduated first in her class, was the valedictorian, and earned a college scholarship. Angeline spoke at one of our fundraisers and said that she looked forward to being the first in her family to break the welfare chain.

A few years ago the world watched in horror as newscasters recounted the events taking place at a high school in Colorado, where two disgruntled students caused untold pain in the lives of so many families. I couldn't help but ponder, *If the two young men who shot their schoolmates at Columbine High School had been in our program, we might have been able to instill in them the sense of self-worth that they were apparently lacking.* Many such youngsters are wounded spirits who need to be healed. Our **KICK**START program teaches youngsters to be a constructive rather than a destructive part of society.

I truly believe that if we can get **KICK**START instituted nationwide in every middle school, we will eventually see a tremendous reduction in gang activity, school violence, and even the need for welfare in our society.

It is my opinion that the advanced moral decay of today's youth began in 1962, when our nation's leaders began interpreting Thomas Jefferson's comments about the "separation of church and state" in a way our country's founding fathers never would have imagined. Prayer was taken out of public schools, and eventually not even the Pledge of Allegiance was required. "God and Country" became an unpopular concept in America's public schools. Added to that, the dress code in many schools was altered to allow students to wear whatever they wanted, no matter how offensive, risqué, or rebellious the outfit.

I believe that many American schools have been on a downhill slide for more than forty years, and it's time we returned to the basics. I'm a strong advocate of strict dress codes for students and teachers. I'm convinced that students do indeed perform better or worse, according to how they are dressed.

I'm even open to the idea of all students wearing uniforms or something similar. As a person who grew up in poverty and was extremely self-conscious about my "rummage sale" clothing, I can attest to the negative effects of never having what the other kids considered normal and acceptable outfits. Perhaps a standard uniform might help many students feel better about themselves. Moreover, wearing a uniform takes away one of the strongest weapons of gang members — their unique outfits. Our youngsters in **KICK**START wear uniforms when they train, and their sense of pride when they have their uniforms on is obvious.

As I was writing this chapter, my thoughts flashed back to Lee Atwater, who was one of the most remarkable men I have ever known. During President Bush's second run for the presidency, Lee was diagnosed with an inoperable brain tumor. His head swelled to the size of a pumpkin. Only certain people were allowed to see him, and I was one of the fortunate ones. I visited him in the hospital just before he passed away. I was standing at the foot of his bed with three other people, when Lee motioned for me to come closer. I stepped to the head of the bed. Lee motioned for me to bend down because he could barely speak. I put my ear to his mouth and heard Lee whisper, "Trust in the Lord, Chuck . . . I love you!"

I kissed him on the forehead and I quickly left his hospital room, desperately struggling to hold back the tears. I made it as far as the car before I burst out crying; I sat behind the wheel and just wept and wept.

It was a sad day for America when Lee Atwater passed away. I believe Lee would have helped make this world a better place. I also believe that had Lee lived and led the charge for President Bush's reelection, the outcome might have been quite different.

For me personally, Lee's passing was not

simply the death of a dear friend; it was also a wake-up call in my own spiritual life. It made the hair stand up on the back of my neck. It hit me that if a person such as Lee, so vibrantly alive, vigorously ripping through life, could be decimated so quickly, perhaps I was not invincible, either. I thought, *I gotta get back on track in regard to my faith and commitment to God. If it could happen to Lee, it could happen to anyone; and you better be right with the Lord when it does.*

CHAPTER 20

Dangerous Moves

I was divorced from Dianne, my wife of thirty years, in 1989. Why our marriage ended after being together that long is a difficult question to answer. Our relationship had survived several rocky periods over the three decades we had stayed together. Now our sons, Mike and Eric, were both grown up and on their own, and one day Dianne and I looked across the table at each other and wondered, *Who is that person?* We had both gone different directions for so long. Although we were on parallel tracks, our lives never seemed to intersect anymore.

I was working constantly, and Dianne had opened a restaurant in Newport Beach, California, that demanded a considerable amount of her time. Her business responsibilities prevented her from traveling with me to my film locations. She ran the restaurant successfully for five years and then decided to sell it. A bright woman with good business sense, Dianne soon started a music production company that demanded even more of her time.

An old saying purports, "Absence makes the heart grow fonder." I don't believe it. The more I was gone, or the more often Dianne's and my business ventures separated us physically, the further we grew apart emotionally. The dissolution of our marriage was not the loud, violent blowout that many couples experience but more like a slow leak that eventually causes a balloon to lose its shape, beauty, and attraction. By the time we realized what was happening, there was nothing left. Dianne was and is an incredible woman, and even though we are no longer married, we remain friends to this day.

Divorce was a shock to my system. Besides the emotional issues of dealing with a sense of failure, I was suddenly thrown into a whole new lifestyle, one I wasn't particularly sure I was going to enjoy. All my life I had been accustomed to being taken care of and nurtured by strong, wonderful women, first by my mom and Granny, and then by my wife, Dianne. I have to admit that I was more than a little scared about being single and alone in

Hollywood. Nevertheless, the thought of being available to the women of Hollywood seemed intriguing. So, I dated . . . and I dated . . . and I dated for about eight months. That's as long as the thrill lasted.

I was making one to three films every year, and by the time each movie was completed, I was drained emotionally, physically, and spiritually. To counter my workaholic tendencies, I recognized that I needed some time away from work for rest and relaxation. Not the type of guy to sit around for long, I wanted to find some activity that would fill the void in my life yet transport my heart and mind away from the workplace for a while.

I remembered Steve McQueen telling me that his favorite form of relaxation was racing a car or a motorcycle since racing required his mind to be totally focused and completely centered on the task at hand rather than on his latest movie. When the race was over, he relaxed thoroughly, mostly from exhaustion! Steve's method sounded like something that might work for me.

Being competitive by nature, I entered a celebrity truck race behind the wheel of a souped-up Nissan in the Frontier 100 Mile Off-Road Race held in Las Vegas, competing against other celebrity drivers, many of whom had been racing for years. Amazingly, I placed first! Not surprisingly, after winning that race, I was hooked.

Soon after that first win, I entered another celebrity off-road race with my son Eric — then nineteen years old — as my codriver. We were in the lead until I rolled the truck over three times. Fortunately, we weren't hurt, but the wreck left Eric and me stranded in the desert for hours!

I had entered and won several more celebrity races when the Vegas race promoters told me they had a ringer to race against me in the Mint 400 in Las Vegas. The night of the pre-race party, a man walked in wearing a racing helmet that covered his face. I stared at him, trying to figure out who he might be. He walked up to me and took off his helmet. To my surprise, it was my brother Aaron!

Aaron is as competitive as I am and had been a stunt driver in many films, so I knew I was in for a real challenge. The following morning, when the race began, Aaron immediately took the lead with me following behind, a close second.

During off-road races there are designated stops where drivers are given beads to prove they have not taken illegal shortcuts. Every time I came to a stop, I'd ask, "How far is Aaron ahead of me?"

The first reply was, "Ten minutes." The second reply was, "Six minutes." The third reply was, "Two minutes."

Aaron later told me that he believed he was way ahead of me, so he slowed down as he got closer to the finish line. He was shocked when he crossed the finish line and six seconds later I came flying through. Steve McQueen was right. The most relaxed I ever felt was after driving that Nissan truck in an off-road race.

In 1985, Michael Reagan, President Reagan's son, broke the world powerboat record from Chicago to Detroit with a time of twelve hours, thirty-four minutes, twenty seconds. In 1989, I was offered the opportunity to break Michael's world record in a race sanctioned by the American Power Boat Association. I jumped at the chance.

I was to drive a forty-six-foot V-hull Scarab boat with twin 425-horsepower engines that reached speeds of seventy miles per hour! The course was 612 miles from the harbor in Chicago to the Renaissance Center in Detroit. My codriver was Walter Payton, famed running back for the Chicago Bears, and the throttleman was Eddie

Morenz. My friend, Bob Wall, came along for the ride.

We left the harbor in Chicago at 7 a.m. and had smooth running over the Great Lakes to Mackinac Island, where we refueled and then took off again, streaking across Lake Huron, headed for Detroit. We were ten miles from the finish line, and within reach of setting a new record, when we encountered a storm that knocked out our navigational system. We got lost in the Detroit channels for more than three hours before finding our way to the finish line. When we finally moored, Walter flopped down on the boat deck and said, "I'll never do this again!"

Undaunted, the following year, I decided to try again to beat Michael Reagan's record. Try as I might, I couldn't talk Walter into returning with me, so I became the lone driver. Eddie Morenz returned as my throttle man, but I did all the driving myself. We had a smooth run, didn't get lost, and arrived in Detroit with a time of twelve hours, eight minutes, and forty-two seconds, bettering Michael's record by twenty-six minutes!

I thought that would be the end of my boat-racing career, but a few months later, Al Copeland, the owner of Popeye's

Chicken, asked me to replace him as the driver of his Popeye Super Powerboat.

I had seen these powerboat races on television and was very impressed. The boats are fifty-foot-long catamarans with jet engines capable of speeds up to 140 miles per hour! A dozen boats race one another around buoys that stretch out over the water for miles. Again my competitive spirit kicked in, so I told Al I would do it.

My first race was to be in Long Beach, California. I arrived on the morning of the race, and Al took me to see the boat for the first time. It looked like a spaceship, much more ominous up close than viewing it on television. I asked Al if I could test-drive it. "Oh, no, I'm sorry," he said. "It's tuned just right for the race. You will just have to go for it."

At race time we pulled out to the starting line and took off. In seconds we were running neck and neck with five other boats, hitting speeds of more than 120 miles per hour! The first buoy we had to go around was about five miles from the start, and as we approached, I told Bobby, the throttle man, that I wasn't sure how to get around it with so many other boats around us. Bobby backed off the throttle, and the five other boats pulled in front of us. Suddenly the boat right in front of me hit a wake and flipped about twenty feet into the air. I barely managed to get around it as the catamaran crashed upside down on the water. When I finally got my heart out of my throat, I thought, *Hey! This is a dangerous game! This will be my one and only race, but at least I can say I tried it.*

We raced hard, and just when it looked as though we had no chance, the two lead boats broke down, and we wound up winning the race! Now I was hooked! I raced superboats nine more times that year and finished the year in third place.

The next year my team and I won the National Superboat Championship. Sadly, Stefano Casiraghi, the husband of Princess Caroline of Monaco, was killed in one of the races, and his death became international news. He was only thirty years of age. I was under contract with Cannon Films, and Yoram Globus, my boss, heard about the tragic accident. "Is that the kind of racing you are doing?" Yoram asked.

I said, "Yes, it is."

"Not anymore," Yoram said bluntly.

My boat-racing days were over. I had won the national superboat title, and I had broken a world record, so what more could I ask for? (Famous last words!) Well . . .

As I previously mentioned, I've always had an incredible respect and immense regard for the men and women who serve in the United States Armed Forces. As a former Air Force man myself, I know all too well the many sacrifices these men and women make to defend our country and to fight for peace and justice around the world.

That's why when I was invited to fly with the Blue Angels, I again jumped at the chance to live dangerously. I flew with the Blue Angels twice. On my first flight in 1991, Kevin, the pilot, buckled me in and told me, "Chuck, about 90 percent of my passengers throw up."

"Why did you have to tell me that?" I asked him. "The thought never entered my mind until now."

Soon after we took off, Kevin tried to get me to barf by doing barrel rolls and other maneuvers. Sure enough, I felt sick. I pulled out the barf bag, but I knew that Kevin would tell everyone that I threw up, so I swallowed it back down. When we landed, I was white as a sheet, but I didn't throw up!

The next time I flew with the Blue Angels, I asked Wayne, the pilot, not to put me through that ordeal again. He said he wouldn't and he didn't. He asked me if I would like to see how he approached an aircraft carrier for a landing. "Sure!" I said.

Wayne told me over the intercom that he would have to slow the jet down from a cruising speed of 550 knots to a landing speed of 140 knots. To do that he would have to bank the plane hard left, which would give it a G force of about six Gs.

When we banked the jet, I saw a bright tunnel closing to complete darkness, and I blacked out for a moment. When the tunnel finally got bright again, I asked Wayne if he was OK.

"Yeah," he said. "I have a pressure suit on."

"Oh, good," I said. "Can I have a pressure suit, too, next time?"

One day at a White House function, I had the opportunity to meet the Secretary of the Navy. I said, "Mr. Secretary, I have spent two days on the USS *Constellation*. I've been on the USS *Kennedy*, and I've flown with the Blue Angels twice, but my dream is to land on an aircraft carrier."

"Really?" he asked.

"Yes, sir."

He smiled and said, "I'll see what I can do."

About four months later I was invited to go to the Top Gun facility at Miramar, near San Diego, where I was to train for two days to prepare for my ride in an F-14 Tomcat and a landing on the USS *Nimitz*, which was 250 miles out at sea.

When I arrived at the facility, I met several of the Top Gun pilots including the one who would be flying me. His nickname was Maverick. Tom Cruise chose Maverick's handle for the name of his character in the movie *Top Gun*.

On the first day I was to train in water-survival techniques since we were scheduled to fly over the ocean. I was taken to a pool that looked to be a hundred feet long. I was wearing my flight gear and boots that felt like they weighed ten pounds each. I was told to swim to the other end of the pool. I was thinking, *I don't know if I can make it with this flight gear on.* The next thing I knew I was in the pool, swimming for the far end. I barely made it across. I was hanging on to the side thinking, *I can't believe I made it,* when I heard someone shout, "Now, come back!" *Oh, boy,* I thought, and started to swim back. I got about half way across, when I was so tired that I stopped kicking, and with the weight of the heavy boots pulling me down, I dropped straight to the bottom of the pool. I kicked up to look for help, but there wasn't any. I went down and popped up three more times, thinking, *They're going to let me drown out here!* Finally, I saw a life raft being shoved out toward me.

"Climb into it!" I heard.

I struggled into the raft, using my last ounce of strength.

The next day I went into the altitude chamber with several military officers including an admiral with whom I was teamed. I told him about my water-survival experience. "Ha! You didn't have to do that," he said with a chuckle. "They just wanted to see what you were made of."

"Well, they found out!" I said.

On the third day I was fitted with a flight pressure suit, and I was ready to go. Maverick and I took off from Miramar air base and headed out to sea to land on the *Nimitz.* As we approached the carrier, Maverick decided to do three touch-and-go landings before setting down on the deck.

Following the third approach, Maverick brought the expensive jet in perfectly, bringing it to a stop with plenty of room to spare on the edge of the aircraft carrier. I climbed out of the fighter jet, toured the carrier, and shook hands with about five thousand sailors and Marines. Then I went up on the bridge to meet the captain.

All too soon, it was time to take off for home. As we were heading back to the base, Maverick told me he was going to show me what it would be like to experience an aerial "dog fight" with an enemy aircraft. He flipped, twisted, and turned the jet every which way. After a few minutes, I felt my stomach doing much the same! I was getting real queasy. I pressed the intercom button, and said, "Maverick, we lost him."

Maverick laughed, and said, "Oh, I get your meaning."

CHAPTER 21

A Sin That Became a Blessing

One morning as I was opening my mail, I came across a letter from a Dianna DeCioli. I opened the letter and started reading, wondering who this person was. I soon found out.

"I am your daughter," the letter said.

The words nearly floored me.

"My mother is Johanna," the writer stated, a woman that I had known many years ago. Dianna went on to say that she was an adult now, married, and had a young daughter of her own. She expressed a desire to meet me to obtain a more accurate medical history. She closed the letter by saying that if I didn't contact her, she would never bother me again.

My thoughts flashed back to August 1962, a week before I was to be discharged from the US Air Force. I was stationed at March Air Force Base in Riverside, California. My brother, Wieland, had come to Riverside to keep me company until I was discharged. My wife, Dianne, was in Los Angeles getting our apartment ready for us to move into when I came home from the service.

One night Wieland and I decided to go out and have some fun. We went to a nightclub where a band was playing and lots of people were dancing. We sat down at a table and ordered a drink, just as a dance contest was announced.

Wieland, who was an incredible dancer, asked an attractive girl at a nearby table to dance with him. They danced up a storm and won the contest! Their prize for winning the contest was free beer for the night.

Wieland brought his dance partner and another girl over to our table and introduced them to me. His dance partner was Joyce, and the other young woman with long auburn hair was her older sister, Johanna. The four of us danced the night away.

Wieland and I took the sisters out a couple times that week and dated them several more times over the next few months. To my shame I never told Johanna that I was married. One night Johanna and I went to a drive-in movie alone, and we engaged in sexual intercourse, right there in the car. It was the first and only time we were sexually intimate.

Although Johanna and Joyce were great girls and fun to be with, I knew that from an ethical, Christian perspective, what I was doing was wrong. It would be an understatement to admit that I felt guilty about being unfaithful to my wife and not being honest with Johanna. It was a situation that I knew must end, so I stopped seeing Johanna.

That had been many years ago. Now suddenly it seemed as though it were yesterday, as I stood reading a letter from a woman claiming to be Johanna's daughter. When I snapped out of my trance, I stared at the letter for a long time, wondering what course of action I should take. The return address on the letter was a town located near my mother's home, about seventy miles away from mine. I called Mom and read the letter to her.

"What do you want to do, Son?"

"Would you call Dianna and talk with her, and let me know what you think?" Mom did better than that. She agreed to a face-to-face encounter with the young woman claiming to be my daughter.

Mom invited Dianna to her home so they could meet. That afternoon I sat by the phone anxiously waiting for Mom's report. When the call finally came, Mom was brief and to the point. "I want you to come over to my house right now. Dianna is here." She and Dianna were waiting for me.

I had no idea what to expect, so I asked my brother Aaron to go with me. As we were driving to Mom's house, I asked myself, *How will I know if she really is my daughter?*

When we arrived at Mom's house, I was nervous, anxious, and scared. I walked into the living room and nearly had my breath knocked out of me. There, standing before me, was a beautiful young lady. I was stunned, but the moment I saw her, I knew. I didn't need DNA or blood tests; there was no doubt in my mind that she was my daughter. I went to her, wrapped my arms around her, and we both started crying. At that moment it was as if I had known her all of her life.

Later Dianna told me how her mother had gotten pregnant from that one and only encounter, and when she was born, her mother named her Dianna but called her Dina (pronounced "Deena"). Johanna got married soon after Dina was born, so Dina always believed that the man her mother married was her father. Johanna never mentioned a word otherwise and probably wouldn't have disclosed the fact that I was her biological father had it not been for an idle conversation when Dina was sixteen.

Dina came home from school one day and overheard her mother talking about me with a friend. "Chuck Norris? What does he have to do with us?" Dina wanted to know. Johanna later confirmed to Dina that I was her biological father but that I was married and had children, and she shouldn't disrupt my life.

Ten years later Dina read in the newspapers that I was divorced. It was then that she decided to write to me with the approval of her husband, Damien.

Dina and I had to cut our visit short because I was scheduled to leave for Israel to begin work on a new film. We assured each other that we would catch up when I returned. While I was in Israel, however, Damien's company transferred him to Dallas. Dina later told me that she was most upset about the move because she felt that after finally finding her real father, she would rarely get a chance to see me, if at all.

As is often said, "God works in mysterious ways." While I was in Israel, I accepted the offer to film the TV series *Walker, Texas Ranger* . . . in Dallas. When I learned that Dina and her family were also in Dallas, I was convinced that this was God's plan for bringing us together.

Since that day in Mom's living room in 1991, Dina, Damien, and their three children, Gabrielle, Dante, and Elijah, have become a blessed part of my life. I have also spoken with Johanna several times, and have apologized for my deceit.

"A lot of time has gone by, Johanna, and I can never bring back the years," I acknowledged. "I wish I could have helped you more at the time of Dina's birth. We were so young, and I had nothing to offer you. But I can help you now, and if you will allow me, I'd like to make restitution and try to make it up to you and Dina. I know I made a lot of mistakes in the past. I'm truly sorry. Would you please forgive me?"

"Yes, of course, I forgive you," Johanna said. "And I know that God has forgiven us. But if it had not been for that night,

Dina would not be here, and I can't imagine my life without her."

Certainly, I know now that God does not condone premarital or extramarital sexual relationships. But I've also discovered that there is no such thing as an "illegitimate child." Every baby is "legitimate" in God's eyes; every child is precious in his sight. Our actions that brought about that baby were wrong. But Johanna was right. Dina is an incredible person, and I am blessed to have her as my daughter, and Damien, her wonderful husband, as my son-in-law. Gabrielle (Gabi) is an angel. Dante is all boy, and Elijah (Eli) calls me "Paka." As a baby, Gabi had mispronounced "Papa," and the name stuck. To this day my grandchildren on Dina's side of the family still call me Paka.

Most heartwarming to me, from the first time we met, Dina called me Dad. My sons, Mike and Eric, have accepted Dina as a sister, just as she has accepted them as her brothers. Today we are one big, happy family. My sin was horrible, but God took what Satan intended for evil and used it for good. As Johanna said, "It was a sin that became a blessing."

CHAPTER 22

Walker, Texas Ranger

While I was in Israel filming the movie *Hellbound*, in 1992, my manager, Mike Emery, called and asked if I would be interested in doing a weekly TV series with CBS called *Walker, Texas Ranger*, a modern-day story of a Texas Ranger with old-fashioned values who champions right over wrong. At first, I was reluctant, but Mike piqued my interest when he told me that the series would be about a cowboy-type law officer fighting crime in a modern Texas city.

"Let me think about it, Mike. I'm not really sure I want to do television," I said. "After all, it would be a big gamble, and if the series isn't successful, it could adversely affect my film career."

But the thought of playing a Texas Ranger intrigued me. When I was growing up, my favorite movies were Westerns. Their overriding message was the Code of the West — friendship, loyalty, and integrity — values I felt ought to be reflected in a television series. I decided to take the risk of jumping from a movie career to television.

I believe that the public wants and needs heroes, a John Wayne–type, American hero. Many people, especially youngsters, want someone with whom they can identify, a man or woman who is self-reliant, stands on his or her own two feet, and is not afraid to face adversity. I decided that if I was going to do a series, this should be the one. My personal beliefs became the core traits of the lead character in the television series, Cordell Walker.

I began filming the *Walker* series in January 1993 and had completed only four episodes when Cannon Films, the company paying the lion's share of the production costs for the series, went bankrupt, and the series was shelved. It was a sad time for me because I really enjoyed doing the show.

Fortunately, about four months later CBS decided to cover the full cost of producing the series, something that is rarely done nowadays. Most television shows are financed by outside groups and sold to the networks for airing, but CBS was so convinced that *Walker* had potential, they were willing to take the risk.

Before long I resumed filming and took on the role of executive producer as well. I brought my brother Aaron on as my coexecutive producer. Aaron had become an accomplished movie director and producer by this time. More importantly, Aaron and I had the same heart, the same attitude. He understood what I wanted to do. My son, Eric, was the stunt coordinator and later became one of my best directors.

I never worked harder in my life than I did those first few years of *Walker*, putting in sixteen-hour days, at least six days a week, and often seven. Each week Aaron and I worked right up until the moment we had to deliver the program to CBS, still fine-tuning and editing. We took a short break around Christmastime, and then we were right back on location in Dallas, filming in the cold weather as well as the searing hot summers. We were writing the scripts and producing what we felt was a mini-movie every week on the *Walker* set. It was a wonderfully creative but exhausting time in my life, but the fans of the program loved *Walker, Texas Ranger,* and that kept me going. *Walker* became the most successful Saturday night series on television since the legendary Western, *Gunsmoke*.

Not surprisingly, many television critics skewered *Walker* as being too violent. I was disappointed but not upset. We had an old-time cowboy feel to our show, and our characters frequently got in fights and fired guns. And of course, *Walker* won a lot of altercations by incorporating his knowledge of the martial arts. That made us a violent show to some people. What the critics chose to ignore, of course, was the fact that the good guys on *Walker* never used violence if there were any other means of apprehending the criminals, and even then we always showed the violence being used as a last resort and as a means of good conquering evil.

Despite being panned by the critics, the public embraced *Walker, Texas Ranger*, and soon *Walker* was not only a well-established program on CBS; it became one of the top-rated shows on television. Maybe that's the reason Peter Jennings, star of the ABC television network news programs, asked me to take part in a special program highlighting the problems in our schools. When Peter invited me to come to Washington,

D.C., he said, "We know that you have a foundation that works with at-risk children. We're going to have children from various schools across America in the audience, and we're going to talk about what's going on in the schools. We're going to have several celebrity guests, including Janet Reno, a female rap singer, and a psychologist. We'd like you to come and talk about the problems in schools but also to talk about how your foundation is helping to solve some of those concerns."

I was working sixteen-hour days on the set of *Walker*, six days a week, and I really didn't have time in my schedule to do the program. But I thought, *I have to do this. It would be a great opportunity to introduce our* **KICK**START *program to America to let people know how successful the program has been and what tremendous results we are seeing in the lives of kids in the Texas schools.*

I rearranged my entire shooting schedule so I could take the day away from the show, fly to Washington, and be on the Peter Jennings special.

The set was divided into four sections, with each guest in a section and the kids sitting on bleachers among us. Peter Jennings began his introductions with Janet Reno. "And we are delighted to have with us today, the esteemed US Attorney General, Janet Reno. Thank you, Attorney General Reno, for being here today." He introduced the psychologist and the rapper.

Peter then turned toward me and said, "And I would like to introduce Chuck Norris, who has the most violent program on television."

That was my introduction.

I realized instantly that I had been set up, that I'd walked into a trap again, similar to the one I had encountered with Phil Donahue years earlier. Peter Jennings wasn't interested in how **KICK**START could help kids raise their self-esteem, get off drugs, get out of gangs, and start living productive lives. He obviously had an entirely different agenda from the one he'd proposed to me in asking me on his show.

I wasn't going to sit back and allow his statement to go unchallenged. I didn't know if it was my turn to talk or not, but I jumped right in. "I'd like to rebut that, Peter. If you ever watch the show, which I doubt that you do, you'd see that *Walker, Texas Ranger* deals with good versus evil. *Walker* is a family show, and if you went through our mail from viewers, you'd realize that families are sitting down together on Saturday night to watch this show and that *Walker* is one of the few programs on television that families *can* enjoy watching together."

That set the tone for a virulent hour of discussion between Peter, the panel, and the audience. When Peter asked one young woman on the bleachers her opinion concerning the violence on television, she responded, "We know the difference between reality and the movies. If you don't, you're really stupid!"

Peter didn't ask that young woman any further questions. He really started to get hot, as the discussion turned in a direction he hadn't anticipated. It got worse yet when Peter Jennings introduced a rap song with sleazy, violent lyrics, in an effort to illustrate the pernicious material being recorded by rappers. As the song played over the speakers, the female rap music artist just sat there, staring straight ahead.

When the song ended, she looked up at Peter Jennings, and said, "Peter, that's not me. That's not even my song. That's somebody else!"

The production department had made a mistake; they'd literally gotten the wrong music from the wrong rap artist as an illustration. Peter Jennings was flabbergasted.

"What do you mean that's not you?"

"That's not my music," the rapper repeated.

I could see heads rolling in the ABC production department.

I can't say that I was sorry to see Peter Jennings so thoroughly discredited in front of his own audience. In a way it served him right for attempting to stack the deck to support his own prejudices, a procedure that is extremely common on most network news programs and the supposedly "unbiased documentaries" on television today. That's one reason many conservative leaders refuse to engage in the programs: the utter bias of the host precludes a fair representation of the issues. On the other hand, that's also why programs that do make an honest attempt to present both sides of an issue are thriving.

I felt no great sense of glee over Peter's embarrassment; I was too angry at him. I was thoroughly disgusted that I had allowed myself to be pulled away from my work and to be lured to Washington on false pretenses. I had come to promote something wonderful, good, and wholesome, and we had hardly talked at all about **KICK**START and the ways it could help kids.

I decided that from now on I'd make my own publicity for **KICK**START, and when people realized the good that can be done in schools, they would rally to our side. Every life matters to God, so every life must matter to us.

I had one goal in mind with *Walker, Texas Ranger.* I wanted a show that the entire family could watch — a show with enough action for dad but not so much violence that children shouldn't watch. Also I wanted to portray good, healthy relationships between men and women and clean humor, so women, especially moms, could enjoy the shows, too.

I believe we accomplished that goal with *Walker, Texas Ranger.* One of the highlights of our run at CBS was the chance to inject several faith-based episodes into primetime. Getting spiritual content on television nowadays is not nearly as difficult as it was in the past. Today's television producers and network executives are quite open to spiritual concepts. Consequently, there are all sorts of weird religious cults and "out there" characters on television. But getting Judeo-Christian values — biblically based ideas, characters, and story lines that accurately reflect wholesome morals and a biblical worldview — on television is another problem entirely.

That's why when we were able to create and air episodes of *Walker* that told a gripping, compelling story that genuinely glorified God, I was extremely pleased. Those programs were some of my most gratifying episodes, and, interestingly enough, some of our highest rated shows! In fact, the first time *Walker* became a top-ten show (a real accomplishment for a program airing on Saturday night), it was a faith-based episode called "The Neighborhood."

The story was about a twelve-year-old African-American girl who lived in the ghetto. While walking home from school one day, she got caught in the middle of a gang war and was accidentally shot and critically wounded.

She is in the hospital when Walker arrives to investigate the incident and is told by one of her doctors that she is bleeding internally, and there is nothing they can do. The little girl is dying.

Miraculously, she recovers, leaving the doctors in total shock. She says that she was on her way to heaven when an angel stopped her and told her that it was not her time; she still had a job to do on earth, to clean up her neighborhood. At the end of the episode, she gets the people in the neighborhood to clean up the graffiti and chase the drug dealers out. At a Christian revival, she convinces the two rival gangs to come together peacefully.

I loved that episode, along with many more that were similarly close to my heart and reflected my faith in God. I've never been a Bible-thumper, but in subtle ways, when the opportunity was available, I tried to inject a positive message in our programs.

One of our many guest stars on *Walker* was Gary Busey, a sincere Christian who has had some ups and downs in his journey but continues to trust God. During a break from filming, Gary and I began talking about our faith. I told him that my wife, Gena, and I read the Bible together every morning and that the Scripture helps me not only with my spiritual walk but also with my emotional attitude toward life.

Gary said, "That's what the letters of the Bible mean: **B**asic **I**nstructions **B**efore **L**eaving **E**arth."

I had never heard that acronym before, but I said, "You know, Gary, you are absolutely right!"

Over the years we had numerous celebrity guests starring with us on episodes of *Walker*. We had everyone from famous actors such as Stuart Whitman to television stars such as Lee Majors to football and baseball great, Dion Sanders, to country music stars Colin Raye, Leanne Rimes, and Barbara Mandrell.

Bob Green, one of my black belts living in Oklahoma City, called me one day and told me that a friend of his, Tirk Wilder, a country singer, had written a song about *Walker*. The song was called "The Eyes of a Ranger." He asked, "Would you like to see it, Chuck?"

"Sure, send it to me in Dallas," I told him. When the song arrived, I read the lyrics, and thought, *This is great! The writer really has captured what the show is all about.* My next thought was to get country artist Randy Travis to sing the song. Randy is a good friend, and I knew that he possessed a strong belief in God and the kind of values we wanted to portray on *Walker*. Not to mention that he has an incredible singing voice that seemed to be a perfect match for our style of show.

I sent the song on to CBS, saying, "I've found a song that I think will work well as a theme song for *Walker*. I'd like to get Randy Travis to sing it."

CBS responded, "We like the song, but we don't think Randy should sing it. We think *you* should sing it."

"Me? I'm not a singer! Maybe in the shower once in a while, but that's about it. . . ."

"No, we think you should sing it, or else we don't want to use it."

Most actors have a secret desire to sing, and most singers have a secret desire to act, and I'm no different, so I said, "OK, let me go into the recording studio, and see what I can do." I felt sure that once CBS heard how badly I sang, they'd recant and gladly allow Randy to sing the song!

I went to a recording studio in LA to record my vocal parts for "The Eyes of a Ranger." The instrumental background music had already been recorded, so all I had to do was sing my vocals. I felt like I sounded awful as I sang the song, but the producer and engineer were so patient with me and so encouraging, I kept trying to do the song better. On some portions of the song, I spoke the lyrics similar to what Johnny Cash might have done because there was simply no way I could sing them. I guess you could call me a "country rapper."

It took nearly twelve hours for me to record my parts, but thanks to the miracles of modern recording procedures, the song didn't sound half bad! I could hardly believe the voice I was hearing in the studio playback speakers was mine!

CBS loved it, and the song became the theme song for *Walker, Texas Ranger.*

Singing the song in the studio, with the help of modern technology, was one thing, but two years later CBS wanted me to sing the song live for a special New Year's Eve program they were producing. CBS had invited singers from various cities around the nation to sing in the new year, and they wanted me to represent Dallas-Fort Worth. My portion of the special was to be shot live in Fort Worth at Billy Bob's, a large country dance nightclub that received national attention as a result of the 1970s movie, *Urban Cowboy,* starring John Travolta and Debra Winger.

For some reason that I cannot explain to this day, I agreed to do the show. I went to Fort Worth to Billy Bob's, and Tirk Wilder, the writer of the song, brought his band to back me up.

An enormous New Year's Eve crowd had gathered at Billy Bob's, and as I was standing backstage behind the curtain, waiting to go on, I was sweating bullets! I was as nervous as I've ever been! I thought, *What am I doing here? Am I out of my mind?* I was pacing back and forth, kicking myself for ever agreeing to do this crazy thing.

I heard the band playing the introduction to the song, the emcee announcing my name, and the enthusiastic cheers of the crowd. I knew there was no turning back. I walked onto the stage, and Tirk handed me a microphone. I muddled my way through the verses of the song, and Tirk and the band members joined in on the choruses. The crowd went nuts! No doubt, some of their musical tastes had been slightly impaired by the amount of alcoholic beverages they had imbibed, but I appreciated their enthusiastic response nonetheless!

Afterward CBS gave me a tape of my live singing debut. I cracked up laughing when I saw my performance. I had stood on the stage, looking like a deer caught in the headlights; my eyes were as big as saucers as I attempted to sing, hugging that microphone, and singing with a total lack of emotion or pizzazz.

I laughed and said, "OK, that teaches me a lesson. I'm never going to do that again! I'd rather face ten black belt attackers than sing live!" Nevertheless, the Billy Bob's experience was good for me because once again I had done something I had thought I could never do. That in itself made it a worthwhile, fun adventure for me, although I apologize to you country music lovers who endured my debut.

We aired our last episode of *Walker, Texas Ranger*, a two-hour finale, on April 6, 2001. It was an emotional time for all of us as we gathered for a wrap party on the set. Many of the cast and crew had worked together for eight seasons; we were as close to a family as it gets on a television series. As we finished our final day's work together, I spoke briefly to the cast and crew. I didn't dare talk too long for fear that I would burst out crying. There were plenty of tears to go around, anyhow, as we all said our farewells.

As we closed up the *Walker* set, I looked over at my wife, Gena, and said, "Let's go home."

When I began working on the series, I thought that *Walker* had the potential to run for three or four years. Never did I believe it would go for eight years! CBS might have picked it up for a ninth season, but by then, Gena was pregnant, and I didn't want to be tied down for the time that a series demands. Gena was carrying twins, and I knew she would need my help. I could never have imagined in my wildest dreams how much help and prayer Gena and the babies would need!

If you would like to catch any of the 203 episodes, they are being aired on the USA Network Channel. I should also mention that *Walker, Texas Ranger* is the highest-rated syndicated show on the USA Network Channel.

CHAPTER 23

The Total Gym Story

About twenty-five years ago I injured the rotator cuff in my shoulder while doing curls with heavy weights on a bench press. I worked through rehabilitation exercises for about four months, using a series of light weights trying to rebuild my strength, but the shoulder was no better. I was nearly ready to give in to my doctors' opinions and have an operation on my shoulder when I received a telephone call from two guys in San Diego who had a new exercise machine they had developed for rehabilitation exercises.

"We saw something in the news about your injury," one of the guys said, "and before you have an operation, you may want to try this. It's brand-new; we just invented it, and we think it might help you without you having to go through the pain, hassle, and other destructive aspects of an operation."

Because of my visibility in the martial arts community, and later in the film industry, I often received pitches for new products. Some of them were interesting and worthwhile; many were not. But for some reason, when the Total Gym guys called, even though I'd never before met them and knew nothing about them, I felt compelled to consider their new exercise machine. *What do I have to lose?* I thought. *If it doesn't work, I can still have the operation.*

I called my doctor and told him that I wanted to put off the operation for a while. Much to his chagrin, I explained to him that I wanted to try one more rehab machine before going under the knife.

Tom Campanero and Larry Westfall, the inventors of the Total Gym, came to my home in the Rolling Hills section of LA and set up their machine in the house. The machine seemed simple enough, just a series of pulleys on a flat, padded bench press. Rather than using heavy weights or complicated machine settings, the Total Gym incorporates your own weight, as you pull your body along an easy-gliding frame. The angle of the board increases or decreases the difficulty of the exercises. It seemed almost too simple as I watched the guys showing me a series of exercises, but it was clear that the exercises they prescribed provided a serious workout for the areas of the body I was concerned about. I tried the machine, and I could definitely feel its effects.

Tom and Larry encouraged me to start at a low level. "Do the exercises each day for ten or fifteen minutes, keeping the plane of the board at a low level for about three weeks," they said, "and see if it doesn't help your shoulder."

I faithfully exercised on the Total Gym every day, and as I felt the strength in my shoulder increasing, I raised the angle level of the board. Amazingly, within three weeks, my shoulder was completely healed! I called the doctor and cancelled the operation.

As I continued working out on the Total Gym, I discovered that I was getting stronger than I'd ever been before, even when I had been working out with heavy weights. The Total Gym was stretching my muscles and elongating them without pain, almost like a dancer or a gymnast doing full-stretch exercises. My body was becoming more flexible, and I could tell that my arms and legs were stronger than they had previously been. When I grappled and wrestled with students in my martial arts classes, I realized that the strength in my grip was more powerful too. I was astounded. I had worked out with every sort of exercise equipment and weights imaginable, but this simple machine was producing more desirable effects, in less time and with less stress!

I still did my martial arts training and aerobic exercises, and tried to maintain a healthy diet, but from the first time I tried it, to this very day, the Total Gym has been a regular part of my daily work-out routine. Over the years I've tried other machines and methods, but I've always come back to the Total Gym.

The only drawback to the Total Gym was its lack of portability. The Total Gym had been originally designed as a machine to be used in rehabilitation centers, not for the general public. But by 1995, Tom and Larry had nearly exhausted the market for selling the Total Gym to rehabilitation centers. They sold a few machines to gyms, but nobody seemed to know what to do with it.

One day as we were talking about their situation, I asked, "Have you guys ever thought about modifying the machine so it could be used in people's homes?"

"No, not really . . ."

"Well, if you could change the design slightly so it could fold up and be put away in a closet or under a bed, I think you guys could make some good money on this."

"Do you really think so, Chuck?"

"Yeah, I do. I know what a benefit this machine has been to me. I'll bet it could help a lot of other people, too."

"Would you be willing to endorse the product?"

"Sure, I would. Every time I've gone overseas to do a movie or something, you have sent me a Total Gym to work out on. I'd be more than happy to help out."

Tom and Larry went back home and worked on the design of the Total Gym, modifying it slightly so it could be packed away after use. When they brought it to Dallas for me to try, I was as excited as they were! The new machine had all the benefits of the original, without the heaviness. Best of all, it could be set up or taken down in a matter of seconds and stored away in about the same amount of space required for an ironing board. I felt sure the guys were on to something big.

"Great! Now we have to find someone who can market the machine for us," Larry said. They researched the various marketing companies and settled on American

Telecast, a marketing company specializing in infomercials.

The guys said, "Chuck, nobody knows this machine any better than you. Would you be willing to do the infomercial for the Total Gym?"

"Well, I'm happy to endorse the machine, but I hadn't really thought about doing anything on television," I hedged. I was already appearing on my own television program, *Walker, Texas Ranger,* and I didn't want to be over-exposed. But something inside me said, "For these guys, go ahead and do it."

I'm now convinced that God was leading me to become involved with Larry and Tom. I knew that they were quality guys whom I could trust. As devout Christian men, their personal integrity was beyond question. Every morning before their actual workday begins, Tom and Larry start by having a brief prayer session with their employees.

"I don't endorse too many products," I told the representatives from American Telecast, "but for Tom and Larry I'll do whatever it takes."

I was willing to do the infomercial for free because of my friendship with Tom and Larry, but American Telecast wouldn't hear of it. "No, we need to work out a contract arrangement of some sort," they said.

"OK, whatever you want to do is fine with me." We struck a deal in which I would make a small royalty on the infomercial sales of the Total Gym.

American Telecast felt that we could appeal to a broader audience if we included a female on the program, so they brought in Christy Brinkley to assist me. I hadn't known Christy prior to filming the infomercial, but she is extremely articulate, cooperative, and wonderful to work with. We had a great time putting together the program.

More importantly, the product was something that we really believed in. I've never endorsed a product I didn't have absolute confidence in, and I couldn't have done the infomercial if I hadn't been convinced of the Total Gym's effectiveness for anyone willing to put in the time and effort, even beginners.

It's always nice to see good things happen to good people. When the infomercial began airing on television stations across the country, Tom and Larry — who had been struggling to find a market for their machine for more than twenty years — suddenly had a new problem.

Sales started pouring in so rapidly that Fitness Quest, the manufacturer of the machines, could hardly keep up with the orders! To date, sales figures on the Total Gym have surpassed a billion dollars! Christy Brinkley and I have done several editions of the Total Gym infomercial. It is the longest-running infomercial featuring a piece of exercise equipment in the history of television commercials. And it's still going!

The Total Gym is so effective it can be deceiving; it works even when you don't realize it. When my son-in-law Damien and family came to visit at our ranch in Texas, he asked if he could work out with me.

"Sure, glad to have you," I said.

Damien watched as I worked out on the Total Gym at the top level. When it came his turn, I placed the bench at a low level, two steps up from the bottom. Damien did the routine with relative ease. He wanted to keep on working out on the Total Gym, but I was a little concerned.

"Damien, you shouldn't go too hard. You don't want to overdo it."

"Oh, no, I'm fine. I can do lots more."

"I'm just telling you that you're going to be sore tomorrow because you've never done this kind of workout before. You're working muscles that you've never challenged before. You're using a lot of muscles at the same time. This isn't like working with a barbell or something."

"No, I can do it!"

"OK . . ."

Damien continued working on the Total Gym and was enjoying every minute, even though he was doing more than I wanted him to do.

The next morning Damien could hardly raise his arms high enough to brush his teeth! He had to lower his head to the sink to get the toothbrush into his mouth.

"I tried to warn you!" I told him with a laugh.

"I'll listen to you next time, for sure," he responded.

Although I've never really used it for that purpose, I discovered that the Total Gym was also effective at helping a person lose weight. I was on a popular call-in radio show hosted by Kid Craddock in Dallas one day when a guy called in and said, "Chuck, I'm using one of your Total Gyms."

"Oh, really? How do you like it?"

"I want to thank you so much," he said.

"Since using the Total Gym, I've lost more than seventy pounds!"

I now have three Total Gyms in my exercise room at home and still use the machine as a regular part of my exercise regimen and plan to use it for the rest of my life. The beauty of the Total Gym is that if it is used according to the instructions, it will provide a vigorous workout for both beginners and people who have worked out for years.

Beyond the benefits I receive from exercising on the Total Gym, the success story is a tremendous illustration of God's faithfulness. Larry and Tom gave Total Gyms to me when they were receiving nothing in return. Then I was able in some small way to be a part of God giving back to them "pressed down, shaken together, and running over."

The only other infomercial I've done to date is for a product called Max.com, an Internet service provider (ISP) that actually filters and blocks the pornography before it gets to your computer and alerts parents when their children are trying to access sites that may not be in their best interests. It is an incredible Internet service provider, and I am proud to be a part of it.

I did the infomercial in 2003 with Patricia Heaton, costar of the hit television show *Everybody Loves Raymond*. Patricia is a sincere Christian woman who, like me, is sick of the smut and perversion being brought directly into our homes, uninvited, by purveyors of Internet porn. Patricia is the mother of four boys, so the protection is especially important to her and her husband, David Hunt. "If our boys can't hack through this thing, I'll know it works," Patricia said.

We tried other blocking programs and discovered that within two clicks of a mouse, one could escape the blocking system and be right back into a porn site. Not so with Max.com. When Patricia was convinced the program really worked, she signed on to do the infomercial.

I appreciate Patricia's concern for integrity and her high standards. I applauded when she walked out during an awards program in which the Osbournes spewed forth a litany of profanity from the stage. "I'm not going to sit here and listen to that sort of garbage," Patricia said, as she left the auditorium.

Amen, sister!

And we don't need to sit back idly while Internet pornography perverts the minds and saps the time, energy, and money of our youth. To me, fighting against the demeaning obscenity being flagrantly dangled in front of our kids (and adults!) on computers nowadays is a moral obligation stemming from my Christian commitment. How could I do otherwise?

CHAPTER 24

Soul Mates

It may be hard for you to believe, but Hollywood can be an extremely lonely place. Despite the constant hustle and bustle, and the myriad lights artificially brightening the dark skies at night, no amount of hype and hoopla can fill the void in your soul when you are alone.

Nevertheless, during the first few years after Dianne and I divorced, I had no desire ever to get married again. I avoided anything that looked like a serious relationship and poured myself into my work. Then I met an attractive young woman through one of my friends. We began dating and struck up a solid relationship. Yet for some inexplicable reason, it never felt quite right. We stayed together for five years, and we almost got married. I bought her an engagement ring, and we were beginning to make wedding plans when we both realized that we were fooling ourselves. Our relationship lacked the kind of total commitment good marriages demand. We broke up, and I was thrust back in the dating game. But I was alone again and miserable.

For the first few years of *Walker*, I was practically consumed with developing story lines, writing, producing, acting, and editing the program. I returned home after work, grabbed something to eat, and fell into bed most nights exhausted. When I took time to socialize, it was usually on an extremely superficial level.

About that time Larry Morales, one of my best friends, came to Dallas to stay with me while I was filming *Walker, Texas Ranger*. He realized how lonely I was and told me he knew a woman I should meet. "She's beautiful, and you won't be sorry. I'd like to invite her to Dallas, and maybe you can give her a small part in *Walker*."

"For you, Larry, I'll do it," I said.

A few nights later I was having sushi at a restaurant in Dallas, along with family, friends, and my date for the evening. I was nose to nose with my date in deep conversation, when I heard Larry introducing someone named Gena to everyone at our table. When Larry finally called out my name, I looked up for the first time and saw the most beautiful woman I have ever seen.

"Er, ah . . . it's nice to meet you, Gena," I said as the beautiful woman extended her hand, and we shook briefly. I then turned back to my date, but the image of Gena was still in my mind.

After dinner Larry drove Gena to her hotel, and I went home. My date hadn't liked the way I looked at Gena, or maybe she saw Gena's reflection in my mind's eye. She didn't say, and I didn't ask.

Gena came on the set the next day and played a small part on the show. She was fabulous . . . and her acting wasn't bad either! I invited her to dinner that night. As we talked about our lives, she told me that she had two young children, and her entire family — mom, brothers, and sisters — all lived in the High Sierra Mountains in a little town called Chester, California, where Gena was a gun-toting member of the county sheriff's force. She had been married before, and since her husband's departure, she had worked two jobs — as a model and as a deputy sheriff — trying to make a living and to take care of herself and her children.

During the few days Gena was in Dallas,

I discovered that she was not only beautiful on the outside but on the inside as well. She seemed to radiate a love, peace, and joy that I always knew existed, but had rarely experienced in my life. I wanted to get to know Gena better, so I asked her to return to Dallas as soon as possible. She came back a couple of weeks later, and our friendship grew into a dating relationship. Before long I felt myself falling head over heels in love.

Nevertheless, I was reluctant to ask her to marry me. We had both recently come out of long-term relationships, and I didn't think we were ready for such a serious commitment as marriage. I knew I wasn't, anyhow. But I wanted Gena in my life, so I convinced her to come to Dallas for a while to pursue her modeling career.

One of her jobs in Dallas was modeling wedding gowns. I attended the show and was amazed at how Gena modeled one gown, then went backstage, and came right back out wearing another gown, looking equally gorgeous in all of them! One of the wedding gowns had an extremely long train attached, and when Gena stepped around the corner to enter the runway, a flowerpot got snagged on the train of the expensive gown. The flowerpot took a ride on the train all the way down the runway!

When Gena turned around and saw the flowerpot hooked on her dress, she was mortified. But she kept her composure and just kept on walking, dragging the decorative piece behind her.

After the show Gena and I had a good laugh about the incident. "That flowerpot looked so good on that dress, I was thinking about buying it," I quipped.

Gena playfully punched me in the arm as her response to my remark.

Later that night I called my mom and told her about the show. I must have been especially expressive about how beautiful Gena looked in the wedding gowns.

"Are you saying that she would make a beautiful bride?" Mom asked whimsically.

"No comment," I deadpanned. Marriage was not in my plans.

Gena's ten-year-old son, Tim, came with her, but her daughter, Kelley, thirteen years of age and in junior high school in California, balked and bristled at even the idea of moving to Dallas. "Please, Mom! Please," she begged. "Don't make me move away from our hometown. All my friends are here."

Gena's sister, Maureen, has a daughter, Caitlin, who is the same age as Kelley.

"Why don't you just let Kelley live with us for a while?" Maureen suggested. "She could be with her friends and continue school in Chester, and when she's ready emotionally, she can move down with the rest of your family in Dallas."

Gena called me in Dallas and told me of Maureen's idea. "What do you think?" Gena asked.

"I don't know," I replied. "It's going to be tough for her either way. You just have to pray about it, and do what your heart is telling you to do." It was hard on Gena to leave her daughter behind, even in the watchful and loving care of family, but she agreed to give it a try, since Kelley was doing so well in her classes and sports.

Gena brought Tim with her from California, and I picked them up at the Dallas-Fort Worth airport. Gena hugged me warmly, but Tim remained distant. He made it obvious from the start that he was far from comfortable with being there. I couldn't say that I blamed him, being uprooted from the only place he had ever known and living with a man he barely knew. But worst of all, Gena and I weren't married.

I stepped carefully with Tim, avoiding any impression that I was attempting to usurp his father's position in his life. After all, Tim idolized his father. I figured it was going to take some time before he warmed up to me.

My sons were equally slow to accept Gena, until they came to know her. Similarly, Gena had to be as patient with my sons as I had to be patient with her children. Winning over our family members was not going to be easy.

Gena and I are both spiritually oriented people, which — after our initial physical attraction — was part of what endeared us to each other in the first place. Maybe that's why I wasn't surprised when I walked in the house one day and found Gena reading the Bible. "I recognize that Book," I said with a laugh.

"Oh, Carlos! Come sit down. Look what I found in the Bible!" She pointed out the passage she had been reading, and it seemed the words leaped off the page at me. I sat down, and we began to read the Bible together. We've done so almost every day since.

Gena and I set out on a search to find a church family, a place where we could learn biblical truth and grow in our spiritual lives. The Dallas-Fort Worth area has no shortage of great churches; quite the contrary, that part of Texas boasts a spiritual smorgasbord ready to satisfy almost every theological taste. Finding a church would be no problem; finding the *right* church for us seemed like a daunting task.

A friend invited Gena to visit a dynamic church located in a tough, run-down part of Dallas. The pastor, Jerry Howell, was a former rock-and-roll musician who still looked the part, long hair and all. Jerry had a heart for people who were hurting, broken, and downtrodden, and he presented the truth in a way that anyone could understand.

Gena and I visited the church several times and were impressed by the sincerity of Jerry and his wife, Jean. No doubt, they could have served well at any upscale megachurch, but instead, they chose to pour their lives out for the down-and-outers in a rough part of town. The non-denominational church was small and intimate, a few hundred people at the most. We enjoyed attending the church, and Jerry's messages were filled with hope, but we recognized that we weren't "home" yet. It wasn't the place where we were supposed to be. Our hunger for a deeper relationship with God grew more intense.

During the year that Gena and I lived together, neither of us ever mentioned marriage, and although we didn't talk about it, the fact that we were "living in sin" grated against our sense of right and wrong. I knew we loved each other, yet something was missing; there was no complete, irrevocable commitment between us. Either of us could wake up one day and simply walk away. More importantly, as we began attending church and reading the Bible together, we became increasingly aware that God's plan was marriage not cohabitation. Beyond that we recognized that our living together without being married was an awful example for Gena's son, Tim, at a time in his life when he really needed positive role models. For two deeply principled people such as Gena and me, the contradiction between what we believed and how we were living became glaringly apparent. The convenience of living together outside of marriage wasn't worth the discontent.

One evening, while we were sitting on the couch watching television, I blurted out, "Gena, do you want to get married?"

"Why?" she asked.

"Because I love you," I said, "and because I want to spend the rest of my life with you."

"When?"

"The only time I have is during my break from filming at Thanksgiving, six weeks away," I said. "Can you put together a wedding that soon?"

"I haven't said yes yet."

I got down on one knee and said, "Gena, please, will you be my wife?"

She laughed and said, "Yes!"

"Good. You've got six weeks."

Before announcing our engagement, however, I wanted to seek the approval of one more person. I went to Gena's eleven-year-old son, Tim, and asked his permission to marry his mom. I remembered how important it was to my mom that I approve of her marriage to George, and I could imagine how Tim would feel if we just sprung the news on him. Fortunately, Tim approved!

In less than two months, Gena put together a beautiful and spiritually moving wedding. We were married at The North Church in Carrolton, a Dallas suburb, with the ceremony conducted by Pastor Lawrence Kennedy, the pastor who met with us in premarital counseling prior to our wedding date. The counseling was especially valuable to Gena and me, since both of us had been married previously and were bringing a large amount of emotional baggage along with us to our new relationship. Beyond that, we needed to deal with matters of repentance and forgiveness of our sins, and Lawrence helped us understand and work through those issues as well.

We included all of our children in our wedding, as well as Gena's parents, her brothers and sisters, my mother and brother, all our grandchildren . . . we had nearly sixty people take part in our wedding ceremony!

Gena surprised me by having country singer Sammy Kershaw and a few of his band members fly in to sing one of our favorite songs, "You Are the Love of My Life." It was a special moment as Sammy sang the words that so aptly expressed the way Gena and I felt about each other.

For a while, though, I wasn't certain I was going to make it down the aisle of the church. Three days before the wedding, Tim and I were out playing basketball, when I wrenched my back. The pain was so excruciating, I could barely walk! The morning of our rehearsal, Gena took me to Baylor University Hospital, where we spent the entire morning in the emergency room.

The doctors couldn't really do much for

me except to prescribe some heavy-duty painkillers. The medicine enabled me to walk and to function, but I felt as though I was in a daze from the drugs. I thought Gena was serious when she pulled a practical joke in the middle of the rehearsal.

With a church full of people, Gena said, "Honey, I know you love the Total Gym so much, I thought we should exchange our vows on the Total Gyms."

I looked at her as though she was out of her mind, but the ushers quickly brought out two Total Gyms and set them up right in front of Pastor Kennedy.

"Go ahead and get on the Total Gyms, and repeat after me," the pastor said. Gena got on a Total Gym on one side of the pastor, and I got on the one on the opposite side. Pastor Kennedy proceeded to talk us through the wedding vows, as Gena and I attempted to work out on the exercise equipment. It was hilariously funny, and the lighthearted approach of Pastor Kennedy helped ease any tension our families may have had about our wedding.

When Gena and I practiced our kiss during the wedding rehearsal, she had pre-arranged for about twenty people to raise scorecards in the audience, similar to judges scoring an Olympic event. I was glad to see that they gave us a passing score!

The night prior to our wedding, my back was no better. I was in such severe pain, Gena called our friend Dr. Hunt Neuhour for help. Dr. Neuhour drove to his office to secure some pain medication, then came to our home around midnight to administer a shot. I rarely use medications of any kind, so it didn't take much to send me for a ride. The medication worked and helped me get through our wedding day without excruciating pain.

Fortunately, we have the entire wedding on video, and every so often Gena and I love to pull out the tape and revisit those precious memories. The former deputy sheriff of Chester, California, and Walker, Texas Ranger, were now married!

Three days after the wedding, I had to be back on the set of *Walker*, so Gena and I agreed to forego our honeymoon until we could truly enjoy it. When we finally had time to take a honeymoon, we flew off to Bora-Bora.

When we returned, I took special efforts to reassure Tim that I was his stepfather, not his dad. I told Tim frequently, "Tim, I'm not trying to replace your father. I'm your stepfather, not your real father. But that doesn't mean I can't love you like my own son. And I want you to know that I will always be here for you. If you have a problem, please talk to me about it."

Tim was a quiet, intelligent boy but with a definite strong will, almost a rebellious streak. Both he and Kelley were skeptical at first about Gena's and my marriage and their new life. They were suspicious of me because I was a celebrity. They later told me that they thought I was going to treat their mom the way so many other Hollywood personalities have handled their marriages: "When it gets boring, move on." Rather than being enamored with the Hollywood scene, or the fact that I was a well-known television personality in Dallas, for months after Gena and I married, Tim and Kelley refused to tell anyone that I was their stepfather.

Their reticence to accept me in their lives hurt me deeply, but I understood their feelings. I realized that I had to be patient, accepting, and humbly try to express as much love to them as they would allow me, without forcing myself on them emotionally.

Since Tim was living with us, I constantly reiterated to him that I understood what it was like to be living with a stepparent. After all, I had grown up with a stepfather myself. I let Tim know that because of the awkwardness of the situation, I was likely to be more tolerant with him. But the one thing Gena and I refused to tolerate from Tim or Kelley was disrespect. Tim responded well to that, and although he and I had several serious eye-to-eye talks over the years, we never had to deal with any issue pertaining to disrespect.

Gena and I enrolled Tim in a Christian school in Dallas, and he slowly but surely began to come out of his shell. Our security guy, Phil Cameron, became like a big brother to Tim, and we will be eternally grateful for his positive influence on Tim. Before long Tim began to warm up to me.

I prayed often that somehow God would help us to bridge the gap between our blended family members. I could not have imagined how he would answer that prayer.

CHAPTER 25

Diamonds in the Rough

When Gena and I were married on November 28, 1998, the last thing on my mind was having any more children. We already had a large instant family. I had three grown children and nine grandchildren, and Gena had two children, one of whom was a teenager, and the other about to enter the teenage years. Having more babies was not high on our list of things we wanted to accomplish.

Then one day, shortly after our marriage, Gena and I had lunch with Alan Autry and his wife, Kim. Alan was a former professional football player for the Green Bay Packers and had played Bubba on the hit television series *In the Heat of the Night*; he was now the mayor of Fresno. Like Gena and me, and so many other couples nowadays, Alan and Kim had both been divorced, but then they found each other and were now happily remarried.

"Starting a family the second time around is the best thing I've ever done," Alan told us. "When I had children the first time, I was young, immature, and I was obsessed with my career. I didn't take the time during my first marriage to really appreciate the joys of fatherhood, but I do now, and I'm enjoying every minute of it! I'd really encourage Gena and you to consider starting a new family," Alan said, looking directly at me.

On the way home Gena asked me, "What do you think about Alan's comment?"

"Honey, even if we wanted to, it can't happen. I had a vasectomy twenty-five years ago, and the odds of a reversal are minimal."

We dropped the subject of having more children, but then some time later, when I was at my **KICK**START tennis and golf event in Houston, Bernie Koppell, from *The Love Boat* TV series, told me how happy he was having children at an age when many men were ready to be grandfathers.

Then, my manager, Henry Holmes, who

was in his mid-fifties, told me about the fulfillment his son, Benjamin, has given him at this stage in life. I was getting inundated with stories of "later in life" second families!

As I was driving home late one evening, after a long, hard day filming *Walker*, I wondered, *Why am I being bombarded by friends who are in second marriages, having babies, and they are all telling me how great it is?*

When I arrived home, Gena had already drawn a hot bath for me so I could relax while she prepared dinner. As I was lying in the tub, I reflected back to a day several years earlier when I visited my good friend, Burt Sugerman. He and his wife, Mary Hart, who hosts the *Entertainment Tonight* TV show, had just brought their newborn baby boy home. Burt took me in to see their baby. I'll never forget the look on Burt's face as he gazed adoringly at his infant son, AJ. I don't think I had ever seen a happier father!

Burt, who has a grown son from a previous marriage, told me that the birth of AJ was one of the most joyous occasions of his life. "Not only do I have a beautiful and wonderful wife and a healthy young son," he said, "but I now have the time to give

AJ the love I feel in my heart."

After I finished my bath, I dressed, walked into the kitchen, put my arms around Gena, and said, "If it were humanly possible, I would love for us to have a baby together."

Gena looked up at me and said nonchalantly, "I have already done a lot of praying and research about this. Would you be willing to fly to Houston to talk to a specialist about your vasectomy?"

"I'm willing to talk to him, but I don't think it will do any good."

Gena smiled. "Let's put the matter in God's hands," she said. "If it is meant to be, it will happen."

Gena and I flew to Houston to meet with Dr. Larry Lipshultz in his office. While we were discussing our situation, I pessimistically told Dr. Lipshultz that I didn't believe a reversal would work because I'd had a vasectomy twenty-five years ago.

"Oh, no," he said. "I don't plan on performing a reversal. I'm going right into your epidymius and extracting the sperm."

"Would you mind repeating that?" I asked.

"If I can't get enough sperm out of your

right testicle, then I will go into your left testicle."

Once I got over the shock of what he meant, I managed to mumble, "Are you sure this will work?"

"Oh, yes," he said. "It's a new procedure, but I feel very confident. The procedure is called MESA, Micro-Surgical Epididymal Sperm Aspiration."

I asked the doctor to explain in plain English what he was talking about.

"I will make an incision into your scrotum exposing the epididymis, the tubules immediately adjacent to the testicles that collect the sperm. Using an operating microscope, an incision is made into these tubules and sperm is aspirated."

"Oh," I said, nodding as though I understood. I had no clue what the doctor was planning, but it didn't sound like much fun. Nevertheless, I had said that I'd be willing to do almost anything. . . .

In December 2000, I went to have the procedure done. I was nervous as could be but didn't feel a thing. Afterward Dr. Lipshultz said, "You did great! And you had all that we needed."

On January 1, 2001, Gena started taking fertility shots every day to stimulate her ovaries to produce multiple eggs. During the month she made several trips to her doctors in Houston so they could monitor her progress. They told her she was doing remarkably well.

A month later the eggs in Gena's ovaries were mature and ready for harvest. The egg aspiration procedure was performed, and fifteen eggs were retrieved from Gena. Of the fifteen, eleven were considered viable enough to attempt ICSY, Intra-Cytoplasmic Sperm Injection. Of those eleven eggs six were healthy embryos. The doctor told us that Gena needed to do the embryo transfer the next day.

When Gena and I arrived at the hospital, her doctor suggested that all six embryos be implanted in her uterus to increase her chances of pregnancy. Gena and I went into another room to discuss our options. If six embryos were implanted, our chances of having one baby would increase, but so would our chances of having multiple births. We were hoping for one baby; two would be great, but six? We decided four embryos would be all we could handle. The nurses prepared Gena for the implantation and wheeled her into surgery. I wasn't allowed to go with her, so I sat nervously watching the clock in the waiting room.

While Gena was in the operating room, the nurse told her, "I want to show you something." She wheeled Gena to an incubator where the four embryos were kept and gently opened the door. The incubator was bathed in warm light and soft classical music. Gena later told me it was the most incredible sight she had ever seen. "It was like looking at something from heaven."

The four embryos were implanted directly into Gena's uterus, and she was brought back to the recovery room. At the end of the day, I was allowed to take her home, where she had to lie flat in bed for three days to give the embryos every opportunity to take.

At first everything seemed to be going well, and we were basking in the wonders of God's wisdom in the way he created our reproduction systems and the advances of modern science, making possible such unusual procedures. But then, eleven days after the implantation, Gena noticed her abdomen starting to swell. She called her doctor, who told her to come to his office right away. He examined Gena and said he believed she was experiencing what is called OHSS, Ovarian Hyper Stimulation Syndrome.

Gena was admitted to the hospital, and

emergency tests revealed that she was, indeed, experiencing a severe case of OHSS. The good news was that a blood test confirmed that she was pregnant, as well. "But OHSS could be very dangerous for you and your child," the doctor said, "so you must follow my directions and remain on complete bed rest. It could take weeks for the complications to pass."

During the next few days, Gena's stomach swelled up with so much fluid that she looked eight months pregnant. The doctor said her ovaries were the size of footballs, full of blood and cysts. He told Gena that she had two options: she could wait it out and see if the OHSS corrected itself, or she could abort the pregnancy.

Abortion was not an option to Gena and me. We believed that if God blessed us with this pregnancy, he would see us through this difficult time.

Three weeks later we went to see Doctor Karen Bradshaw, Gena's obstetrician, for a sonogram. Dr. Bradshaw started moving the sonogram over Gena's stomach to check for signs of the baby. We were looking at the screen with her, when she said, "There's that little tyke." Then she moved the sonogram upward, and said,

"Wait! There's another one!"

"Wow," I said, gulping hard, and taking a deep breath. "Twins!"

Then she moved the sonogram to the left and said, "There might be another one."

"Triplets? Are you sure?" I had to sit down on that one.

"No," she said. "We'll have to wait a week to see if you are going to have two or three babies."

During the week all I could think about was: Are we going to have twins or triplets? If Gena gives birth to triplets, how are we going to rock and feed them at the same time? How does a family with four or five babies care for them all at the same time?

The week passed, and the question was answered. We were having twins. I breathed a sigh of relief. Two babies we could handle!

During the weeks that followed, Gena remained confined to her bed. She needed oxygen to help her breathe, and a nurse came by each day to take her vitals and draw blood. Another nurse came at night to make sure that she remained stable. The nights seemed to be the hardest on Gena.

Since her movement was extremely restricted and throwing a big party was out of the question, for my birthday Gena arranged a spa treatment package for me. It was a wonderful gift in more ways than I could ever have imagined. I climbed on the table, stretched out, closed my eyes, and the masseuse went to work on me. I was so relaxed I almost drifted off to sleep, right there on the table.

But then it happened. I had a strong premonition that Gena and I were going to be having a boy and a girl and that the boy would be named Dakota Alan and the girl Dani Lee. Alan was after my father-in-law, and Lee was after my mother. At about the fourteenth week, we found out through one of the ultrasounds that our twins were indeed a boy and girl.

During the following weeks Gena's condition seemed to improve; her left ovary was returning to normal, but her right ovary remained enlarged. A specialist explained that such a problem could be life-threatening to Gena or the babies and talked of removing her right ovary while she was pregnant. He said if her condition did not improve by the twentieth week of the pregnancy, the ovary must be removed. We prayed constantly that God would intercede, even if it meant performing a modern-day medical miracle.

Our prayers were answered! By the twentieth week, both ovaries had shrunk, and the surgery was no longer necessary.

When Gena told my stepdaughter Kelley what we were going to name the babies, her reply was, "I think Kelley should be somewhere in my baby sister's name." We talked about it, and agreed with Kelley. We changed the name Dani Lee to Danilee Kelley Norris.

Steve Scott, a close friend and board member of my **KICK**START Foundation, told me that when his wife Shannon had experienced difficulty with her pregnancy, he took her to see Dr. Greg Devore, a leading perinatologist in Pasadena, California. He believed Dr. Devore was responsible for saving their baby.

Gena was happy with the hospital and the doctors in Texas, but I couldn't get Steve's comment out of my mind. You could call it an instinct, but I believe it was God's Spirit telling me that Gena needed to be near this particular doctor, just in case another emergency should arise. When I told Gena that I felt strongly that we needed to be near Dr. Devore, so we were moving to our house in Los Angeles and having the babies there, she was not happy with the news.

Quite the contrary! Gena cried and cried. She loved her doctors and wanted very much for our babies to be born in Texas. Besides, she'd have to find a good obstetrician who could take care of her and deliver the babies in California. I explained as best I could about the premonitions I was sensing, and reluctantly, she agreed to go. So, with Gena in her twentieth week of pregnancy, we moved to Los Angeles.

Once in LA, Gena was able to find an obstetrician who was just minutes from our house, as well as a nearby hospital. She also started to see Dr. Devore regularly.

At twenty-three weeks into her pregnancy, Gena started feeling some pressure in her cervical area and began experiencing contractions, but she dismissed the discomfort as an aspect of carrying twins.

That same week I was scheduled to go to Washington D.C. for President Bush's first White House dinner. "Oh, go ahead. Don't worry about me," Gena said sincerely. "I'll be fine. You and the guys go and enjoy the celebration."

I invited my brother, Aaron, and our friends, Dennis Berman and John Hensley, the former head of US Customs, to join me for the presidential gala. Phil Cameron, my personal protection officer, joined us as well.

While I was in Washington, Gena was scheduled for her regular appointment to see Dr. Devore. She considered canceling her appointment, but she felt something was just not right. She drove herself to the appointment with Dr. Devore.

When Gena explained to Dr. Devore about the unusual level of discomfort she was feeling, the doctor was concerned. He immediately examined her cervix with an ultrasound and checked the babies. When he finished the exam, the doctor appeared perplexed. He explained to Gena that Dakota's heart was working too hard and was developing fluid around it. He also expressed concern that Gena's cervix was beginning to soften. She was going into preterm labor. "Gena, we need to admit you to the hospital right away," Dr. Devore said. "We must surgically insert a cerclage, basically to sew your cervix closed." Dr. Devore explained, "The babies are not yet viable, weighing approximately one pound each. If you go into labor, the babies probably will not survive."

CHAPTER 26

Miracle Babies

Pacing the floor in my Washington hotel room, I could hardly stand the wait. I was angry at the copilot for taking a drink, although it really wasn't his fault that I was stranded in D.C. The pilots hadn't planned on returning to Los Angeles until the morning following the presidential dinner. That was before we found out about Gena being in the hospital, facing some tough times ahead of her.

When I talked with Gena that night, I assured her that I would get home as quickly as possible, so the moment the pilots were able to fly, we took off and flew directly home. I prayed all the way home that God would spare our little Dakota and Danilee.

The morning of the surgery, Gena's doctor explained a further possible complication to her. There was a chance that the amniotic sac the babies were in could rupture, which would result in her losing the babies. Frightened, Gena began to pray, asking God for a miracle. Once again our prayers were answered, and the surgery was a success!

Following the surgery, Gena was ordered to full-time bed rest, not an easy thing for my active wife. She could get up only to shower and use the bathroom and was given a device to be worn around her abdomen that read her contractions twice a day. A nurse visited Gena twice a week to listen to the babies' hearts.

During the twenty-seventh week Dr. Devore noticed fluid developing around Danilee's heart. Danilee had an abnormally vascilating heart rate, alternating between an extremely high rate, then dropping to a very low heart rate. Dr. Devore was concerned and said he would need to keep a closer eye on the twins.

Gena's belly had gotten so big and she was so miserably uncomfortable that she focused only on getting through the day; anything else was too much to handle. We did a lot of Bible reading, which helped keep us strong and encouraged. When she wasn't studying the Scripture, Gena read every medical book she could get hold of that contained information about multiple pregnancies.

Danilee's heartbeat was still irregular, but we knew she was a fighter. She moved constantly inside Gena; that little girl never slept! Sometimes at night, while Gena was trying to sleep, I'd lay my hand on her belly, and I could feel a kick here and a push there. The twins' movements were distinctive, too. Dakota didn't move nearly as much as Danilee, but when he did, it was with such great strength that we knew he meant business. He probably was tired of his sister pushing him around!

Gena began seeing Dr. Devore twice a week. We really looked forward to the appointment since it gave us a chance to watch our babies on the ultrasound machine, not only to make sure that they were doing OK, but to look at all their wonderful, amazing features. The Bible says that God knows us even before we are born and that each of us is fearfully and wonderfully made. I was beginning to understand that even more fully as I followed the weekly growth and development of our children in Gena's womb. Gena and I would make bets on how much each baby would weigh. When Dr. Devore checked Dakota, he always teased us, saying, "It looks like you've got yourselves a football player here!"

As Gena approached her thirtieth week of pregnancy, Dr. Devore informed us that he was getting a new ultrasound machine that would project four-dimensional images. He planned to use it on Gena because it would show better detail of our babies. The new technology turned out to be a lifesaver.

Gena's surgery date was scheduled for October 23, which seemed like an eternity to her. As she rounded into her thirty-first week of pregnancy, Gena developed a sharp pain on her right side. She tried changing positions, but nothing eased the pain. "Maybe the intense pain is because I'm carrying two babies," Gena said, "but I've never had such excruciating pain during a pregnancy before." After five days of enduring the pain, she called her OB. The doctor instructed Gena to come to his office immediately.

He ran blood tests to be sure she didn't have a ruptured appendix and did another ultrasound. "Everything appears to be fine," he said. "Maybe you've pulled a ligament."

That didn't seem likely, but Gena accepted the possibility and came home to begin her thirty-second week of pregnancy, a milestone for her. To OB and neonatal doctors, thirty-two is a magic number. Babies born at that time do much better with fewer serious complications than those born earlier.

Before Gena and I went to sleep that night, we prayed as we do every night. Then Gena said to me, "For some reason I feel a little afraid, and I don't know why, but I want you to know something. If anything happens to me, please, always remember how much I love you and keep Jesus close to your heart."

The next morning Gena noticed that Dakota had stopped moving and that her old Caesarian scar had an unusual look about it; she thought it appeared to be protruding outward. We called Dr. Devore immediately. As the doctor examined Gena on his new four-dimensional ultrasound machine, I saw his eyes widen, and concern creased his face. He explained to us that Danilee now had more fluid around her heart, and Dakota's heart was working way too hard. He ran the ultrasound wand over Gena's abdomen and said, "The babies need to be born right away. Gena's uterus is ready to rupture." Dr. Devore said, "Do not go home, don't go anywhere else, but go straight to the hospital." Shocked and terrified, we rushed to the hospital. Gena cried all the way, saying her babies were not ready to be born. Driving like a maniac, I didn't think we had a choice.

Gena was wheeled into an operating room and prepped for emergency surgery, while a nurse gave me instructions and handed me a blue surgical outfit, complete with a hat that looked like a lady's shower cap and a pair of "footies." I put the outfit on over my clothes.

Meanwhile Gena was experiencing an unusual covering of a different kind. While lying on the gurney in the operating room, a kindly African-American nurse asked softly, "Would you like me to pray with you before your surgery, honey?"

Surprised, Gena barely eked out the words, "Yes. And would you pray for our babies too?"

The sweet woman prayed a simple prayer, asking God to be with Gena and the babies throughout the surgery and to guide the physicians as they performed the procedures. She then led Gena in repeating the Twenty-third Psalm. "The Lord is my shepherd, I shall not want. . . . Even though I walk through the valley of the shadow of death, I fear no evil, for You are with me. . . ."

A short while later I joined Gena in the

delivery room, along with Gena's fourteen-year-old son, Tim, who planned to video-tape the birth of the newest members of our family. Tim was so nervous he forgot to turn the camera on!

When Gena's doctor began the surgery, he confirmed that Dr. Devore was right. "I can clearly see the heads of both babies through the outside of your uterus; it is as thin as a piece of cellophane. It's a good thing you got here when you did."

Watching the birth of our babies was a new and awesome experience for me. When my sons from my previous marriage had been born, I was not allowed in the delivery room. Now I didn't want to miss a moment!

Only a father who has experienced being in the delivery room and watching his baby (in my case, babies) come into this world and hearing the baby's first cry can understand just how overwhelming the joy of such an experience really is. I couldn't keep the tears from streaming down my face.

Dakota was born first. He came into this world with a healthy cry, weighing in at four pounds, six ounces. Danilee was born next, crying loud enough to let the whole world know she had arrived. She weighed three pounds, thirteen ounces. As soon as each twin was born, I cut the umbilical cord, and then they were rushed up to the neonatal unit.

When the doctor finished Gena's surgery, she was wheeled into the recovery room, where I was waiting for her. I hugged and kissed her and told her how proud I was of her. Gena wanted to see Dakota and Danilee, so the nurses wheeled her to the neonatal intensive care unit. Together we peered through the window at our two little miracle babies. Danilee was doing well and breathing on her own, but both of our babies had numerous wires attached to them, intravenous lines inserted into their tiny veins, and a feeding tube running down through each of their noses into their stomachs. The wires were attached to monitors that measured the babies' heart rates and breathing. If a problem were to develop, alarms would sound, alerting the on-duty NICU nurse or doctor immediately.

A couple of days later, Gena and I were finally allowed to hold the twins in our arms. What a blessed experience! But then while I was holding Dakota, and looking down on his beautiful face, the alarm began sounding on his monitor. He had stopped breathing! I almost had a coronary myself!

The on-duty nurse ran over, grabbed Dakota out of my arms, and began lightly shaking him. The alarm stopped. She smiled and put him gently back in my arms. I was still in shock.

"What happened?" I gasped.

"It is not uncommon for 'preemies' to stop breathing," she said. "When that happens, we stimulate the baby and get him breathing again."

The nurse made it sound so routine, and maybe it was to her, but it's not routine when it's *your* baby! It was frightening, and even though we understood why, when it happened, Gena and I were completely unnerved.

Although Dakota was the bigger of the two babies, he was experiencing the most problems. For some reason male "preemies" have a more difficult time breathing. I know it's hard to believe, but their lungs just aren't as strong. Dakota had a moderate case of respiratory distress. He needed the assistance of a breathing unit for five days and had to be fed only through his IV. Finally, he began breathing normally on his own.

Danilee and Dakota were supposed to stay in NICU for at least eight weeks, but after four weeks of living at the hospital,

Gena and I decided to bring our babies home. We arranged for in-home, round-the-clock nursing care.

Danilee and Dakota had to remain on heart monitors for three more months. They were finally taken off the heart monitors just before Christmas 2001. It was the best Christmas present Gena and I could ever receive.

The elation we felt in bringing Danilee and Dakota home was almost indescribable. Multitudes of our friends lavished gifts and well wishes on our babies. One hand-written note was especially meaningful:

Dear Danilee and Dakota,

Your wonderful mother sent me a picture of you two when you came into this great big world. I used to be the president of the USA; now, I'm just a guy who loves his family and his friends. We Bushes love your mom and dad. We are so lucky to have their unconditional love. Welcome to this great big, exciting world. May your lives ahead be full of happiness, love, and wonder.

With all our family's love,
George H. W. Bush

My friends were right. Having children at my age was one of the most exciting and pleasurable times in my life. The first time around, I was too busy trying to make a living, and I missed a lot in the raising of my children. But with my new family members, I was able to be at home and nurture the babies along with Gena.

As the months passed, I watched the babies grow from infants to crawling babies and then to little toddlers, starting to walk and express their personalities. It was an experience that I will cherish for the rest of my life. Now it's up to Gena and me, as parents, to instill in our twins a sense of self-worth, not egotistical pride, but character-building tools based on biblical principles.

Just as we began to relax and breathe easier, we noticed that our fourteen-year-old, Tim, the youngest of Gena's children, was jealous of the attention we showered on our newborns. Tim wanted nothing to do with the twins. Kelley, on the other hand, was instantly affectionate with her new siblings. Often Kelley chided Tim, "How can you not love these babies?"

Tim grunted and walked away from her.

The turning point came when the twins were about six months old. Tim walked by their cribs one day and saw Dakota reaching up for him. Tim was unable to resist. He picked up Dakota and cradled him in his arms. Today Tim is enjoying his role as big brother.

Kelley and Danilee are inseparable. At the end of Kelley's high school basketball and baseball games, she carried Danilee in her arms as she high-fived the opposing team.

Unfortunately, Kelley didn't show the same affection toward me. For almost six years, when I would hug Kelley, she would not reciprocate. All I could do was hope and pray that one day she would love me as much as I love her.

After many of Kelley's games, I would stand back while Gena hugged her. I didn't want to presume upon a special mother-daughter moment, and I didn't want to overstep my bounds as Kelley's stepdad.

I had an important meeting the day of Kelley's basketball championship, so Gena planned to fly up to the game without me. But something inside of me said, *This is important.* At the last minute I canceled my appointment and flew to California with Gena. I knew it was Kelley's last game, and I didn't want to miss it.

Kelley's team lost by four points, and

Kelley was crying from the disappointment, as well as the realization that her high school sports days were over. Gena was hugging her, and as usual, I stood back. Suddenly Kelley let go of Gena and put her arms around me, laying her head on my shoulder, crying. I consoled her by telling her what a great game she had played, but my heart was leaping with joy. This beautiful young lady had finally accepted me as her stepfather!

Thanks to God's grace, Danilee and Dakota have become the glue that binds our two families together. We now have a wonderfully blended family. In fact, my eldest son, Mike, often calls Gena whenever he needs advice. And my grandchildren affectionately refer to Gena as "G-ma," which Gena thinks is wonderful.

CHAPTER 27

Spiritual Surprises

Funny, for years I simply went about my business, going through life, doing my own thing, almost unaware of God's presence in my life or his workings in the lives of my friends. Now that I've traveled a few more miles in my spiritual journey, I'm able to recognize the hand of God in ways I never have before. Amazingly, he has been there all the time, working all around me. I just didn't know it. Sometimes, I've simply had to step back and say, "Whew! I didn't know that God could do such awesome things nowadays, but apparently he can!"

For instance, Ken Gallacher, a close friend and a man of great faith, drove with his family from their home in Las Vegas to Disneyland in Anaheim. Toward evening, after spending a fun day at the park, the family piled into their van and headed for home. They had barely gotten under way when their vehicle malfunctioned on the highway, and they were forced to pull over to the freeway's inside emergency lane. Ken got out of the van, walked around to the front, and opened the hood to see if he could tell what was wrong.

Just then, a drunk driver hit the Gallacher vehicle from behind at a speed of more than seventy-five miles per hour! The van was knocked nearly sixty feet up the highway by the force of the impact, spinning around two and a half times. Fortunately, the family members all were wearing seatbelts. They were badly shaken up from the jolt but were basically OK.

Ken, however, was hit by his own vehicle, the impact catapulting him more than two hundred feet in the air. He literally flew across the freeway into oncoming traffic. A driver approaching from the opposite direction saw the accident happening, slammed on his brakes, swerving his car sideways in front of oncoming traffic. Ken slammed onto the road in front of the stopped car. As awful as that was, at least it kept Ken from being run over by the oncoming traffic in the dark.

Ken was rushed to the hospital, the family fearing the worst. He had suffered severe injuries to his face and head, had three broken ribs, a broken elbow, torn ligaments in both knees, and internal damage to his heart, lungs, stomach, and liver. By the time I arrived at the hospital to be with our friends, Ken's condition was even worse. But a lot of people were praying for Ken, and three days later he miraculously walked out of the hospital under his own power. He had a long road of recovery ahead, but he was alive!

Over the next several months, thousands of dollars of medical bills rolled in, but Ken noticed that he still had not received a bill from one particular doctor. He called the doctor's office to set up a payment agreement, and said, "Doc, I've never received a bill from you for your services the night of my accident."

The doctor replied, "Ken, I cannot bill you for what God did. We literally saw you healed in front of our eyes."

I believe in a God who can do extraordinary things such as that!

I'm still as amazed as anybody when God uses my life to impact someone else in a special way. I've made plenty of mistakes in my life, and I sure don't claim to know all the answers. That's why I was surprised when Pastor T. D. Jakes invited me to speak at The Potter's House, a large church in the Dallas area. The church was packed that night. I was extremely nervous but determined to do my best. Members of the Power Team, a group of Christian bodybuilders, did a tremendous demonstration prior to my presentation. The crowd was really pumped by the time I got up to speak.

Although I attend a lot of celebrity events, I'm not really known as a spontaneous, extemporaneous public speaker. If I have to give a talk, I like to prepare well in advance, thinking through everything and knowing exactly what I plan to say. That's what I did for my presentation that night at The Potter's House too.

The Potter's House congregation is predominantly African-American, and as I stepped up to the podium, the crowd gave me such an enthusiastic welcome, I was momentarily unnerved. Talk about an alive church!

I regained my composure and launched easily into my prepared remarks. Meanwhile, the Power Team sat behind me, praying for me and urging me on. Suddenly something came over me that I now understand to be the power of the Holy Spirit, but at the time I was as befuddled as anyone else. My meticulously planned speech suddenly changed; it just went out the window. I started saying all sorts of things I had never before said to any group, talking about the power of God to change a life. I felt an incredible freedom, and I simply flowed with it.

Behind me I could hear the guys from the Power Team shouting encouragement, "Tell it, Chuck! Tell 'em!"

When I came off the platform, Gena hugged me and said, "Honey, I'm so proud of you!"

"For what? What did I do? I can't remember a thing I said!"

In 1999, Gena and I attended a marriage seminar in Dallas, conducted by Dr. Ed Cole and his wife, Nancy. We had met the Coles briefly at the 1998 Epiphany Awards, at which *Walker, Texas Ranger* had been honored as the Best Christian Program on secular television. In his late seventies, Ed was still a well-known men's conference speaker and a prolific author, including the best-selling book, *Maximized Manhood*. Nancy's health had been failing for some time, yet she remained a stalwart part of Ed's ministry, radiating love and joy to the young couples who attended the seminar. Gena and I were on the older end of the age spectrum of those in attendance, and we had a good marriage, but like a fine automobile that needs an occasional tune-up, even the best marriages can benefit from a fresh look under the hood. Perhaps *because* of our age, we thoroughly enjoyed Ed Cole's seminar and down-to-earth, practical wisdom as much as the young couples.

Before the seminar's conclusion, Nancy's energy level had dropped severely, and she had to go into a back room to lie down. As we were leaving, Dr. Cole said to us, "Nancy would like to say good-bye to you if you have time before you go."

We went into the room and found Nancy lying on a couch, covered with a sweater. I bent down to greet her, and she leaned up to kiss me on the cheek when Gena and I entered. When she did, she noticed that Gena was cold. "Honey, you're so cold," Nancy said. "Here, take my sweater and put it on." We were awed at Nancy's self-less love; there she was, exhausted and chilled, at the very ebb tide of life, and she was still thinking of others. What a woman! That was the last time we ever saw Nancy.

Not long after the seminar, she passed away. We were sad for Ed and shared in his grief, but we all knew that Nancy was in a better place, in the eternal care of our God.

Although we had conversed with Ed and Nancy at the seminar, we really didn't know them. Nor did they know anything about our personal lives. That's probably why we were surprised one rainy day, a few months after Nancy's funeral, when we received a telephone call from Ed Cole at our office, asking if he could come over to meet with us.

I was in the middle of a script meeting, so I wasn't too excited about having an unexpected visit just then. But Gena felt it was important that we see Dr. Cole. "If he wants to drive all the way across town in the rain, there must be a good reason," she said.

Gena and I were accustomed to receiving many requests for our time, charitable contributions, or lending our name to someone's good cause. Wanting to remain open to opportunities as they arise, it's sometimes difficult to know which needs are legitimate and which are simply rip-offs trying to use us for selfish reasons. We've learned that the only two fail-safe methods for discerning the validity of these requests are time and prayer. Taking time to pray through a request is not easy, though, since it drains one of our most precious commodities — time. Maybe that's why we've also developed a healthy skepticism.

Not surprisingly, Gena's first response when she heard that Ed Cole wanted to speak to us was, "Well, he either wants something from us, or he has something prophetic to say to us that we need to hear." Gena had admired Ed Cole for years and was much more aware of his ministry and accomplishments than I was, but I had sensed a genuineness about Ed at the marriage seminar. Although I'm sometimes too naïve and trusting when it comes to discerning people's motives, I felt that I could trust Ed.

"Out of respect for Dr. Cole, let's meet with him," Gena said, "and hear what he has to say."

"Fine, tell him to come on over to the house," I replied.

The rain was relentless that day when Ed Cole came to our home in Dallas. He was drenched and trembling as he came inside and sat down on the couch. I took a break from my script meeting, left the writers in the den, walked into the living room, and sat down next to Ed. After some cordial small talk, Ed got right down to business.

It was obvious that he felt he was on a mission from God.

"You may think I'm crazy, and you may tell me to leave when I share this with you," he said, "because I don't know you well. But God has laid this message on my heart, and I'm convinced that I am to tell you something. How you respond is up to you." Dr. Cole turned to the Bible and read a brief passage to us. His hands were shaking as he held the Book and said, "I just want you to know that there are going to be many people who will come to you, and they will call themselves brothers, but they want to use you for their own personal gain." Dr. Cole went on to explain how he felt that because of our simple, childlike faith, we were vulnerable to be taken advantage of by wolves in sheep's clothing. He encouraged us to get grounded in God's Word, the Bible, so we could tell the difference between the genuine brothers and sisters and the counterfeits.

I was shocked. I'd lived and worked in an extremely competitive world for most of my life; I was acutely aware of the backstabbing, undermining, and wheeling and dealing that goes on every day in the film industry. I was accustomed to dealing with users, abusers, and other losers. But Dr. Cole was clearly implying that we needed to beware of people who came to us in the name of God, whose motives were suspect, and who were seeking only their own selfish aggrandizement. It was obvious that his own words caused him great sadness and pain as he spoke to us.

Dr. Cole visited with us for about thirty minutes; we talked about his wife, Nancy, and how he missed her, and we talked briefly about our family; we hugged Ed, and then he left. He had no sooner gone out the door when Gena was overwhelmed. "Honey, do you realize what just happened here?" she asked. "God used Ed Cole to speak to you and me. He brought him all the way across Dallas in the middle of a bad storm to tell you this message because God loves you so much!"

We didn't hear from Ed for a while, and when we did, the news wasn't good. We received a letter from Dr. Cole in Los Angeles asking us to call him, and to pray for him, that he was bedridden and had been diagnosed with cancer. We called him right away and realized that his condition was worse than Dr. Cole was letting on.

Gena and I decided to fly to Dallas to see him at his bedside. We took my son,

Mike, along with us. Dr. Cole's eyes still danced with light and life, but his body looked feeble and sickly. It was obvious that he was not going to be with us much longer. Nevertheless, he greeted us warmly when we entered his room. We talked for a few minutes, and then my son, Mike, literally dropped to his knees at Ed Cole's bedside. He grabbed Dr. Cole's hand and began praying for our friend.

Mike completed his prayer, and while he remained on his knees, Dr. Cole reached over, placed his hand on Mike's head, and in language reminiscent of an Old Testament prophet, Dr. Cole prayed a blessing over Mike's life. It was one of the most powerful spiritual experiences I've encountered to date. I'm convinced that part of Mike's passion to develop family-oriented, faith-based films is directly attributable to that blessing bestowed upon him by Dr. Ed Cole.

As we prepared to leave, Ed looked up at us and said, "I cannot believe that you love me so much that you'd get on a plane to come see me."

It was the last time we ever saw him on earth. He died a few weeks after our visit, just short of his eightieth birthday. We missed the mighty man of God who had become so dear to us in such a short period of time, but we knew we'd see him again in heaven.

Over the last three decades of his life, Dr. Cole had been a featured speaker at many events encouraging men to trust in God, to be faithful husbands and fathers, to be real men. I recognized that in some ways, he and I were trying to do the same thing. What a legacy he left for me!

CHAPTER 28

The President's Man

Gena loves to make every day special, but she goes out of her way to celebrate my birthdays. One of the most memorable was a birthday "party" she planned for me while I was still filming *Walker, Texas Ranger*. Weeks in advance of the actual date, she started dropping little clues about what we were going to do on my birthday, but I was baffled. She began sending me intriguing notes, similar to a treasure hunt, several days before my birthday. I still couldn't figure out what she had in mind, but I knew it had to be good!

Two days before my birthday, I was working on a scene of *Walker*, when a bag lady walked on the set. Frumpy looking, wearing several layers of clothing, and carrying a large grocery bag, the woman somehow got through our security guards and literally walked right into the middle of a scene while we were filming!

I could hardly believe my eyes! I've had strange situations occur before but never one in the middle of a scene. I once had a female fan claim that she was carrying my baby because she had become pregnant through watching my program on television. She'd even sent photos of the baby! Anyone who has ever worked on television or in movies has their own collection of overzealous fan stories.

"Excuse me, ma'am," I said, trying to be polite but firm. "You can't be here. We're trying to film."

The woman seemed totally unconcerned. "Oh, that's quite all right, sonny. I've come with a special message for you. I must give you something," she said as she attempted to hand her bag to me.

I waved her off. "No, thank you, Ma'am," I said, not sure what she had in the bag. "I appreciate your kindness, but you really must leave." I glanced at our security guys a few feet away and noticed they were ready to put the clamps on her. "I don't want to be rude," I continued, "but we're trying to work here. Fellows, please help this dear woman find her way out."

The security men came over and positioned themselves on each side of the woman. When she protested their encouragement that she leave, the guys simply lifted her up by her arms and carried her off the set, still kicking and screaming.

I just shook my head. I didn't know what to think. A few minutes later the bag lady came storming back on the set, and on the bottom of her bag was another of Gena's clues concerning my upcoming birthday surprise. Everyone on the set that day broke up in laughter; they'd all been in on the joke, everyone except me!

The following day I was back at work on the set when the producer, Gary Brown, came up to me and said, "Gena wants me to blindfold you. Can I do it?"

I looked at Gary and laughed, intuitively knowing that our work for the day was done. "Oh, OK," I responded.

Gary blindfolded me and led me off the set, out the door, and across the parking lot. "Step up, Chuck," Gary said, as he guided me onto a set of narrow steps. I stepped inside a vehicle and sat down, still blindfolded. Suddenly, I heard the unmistakable sound of a helicopter motor. We took off, and the copter whisked Gary and me across Dallas to Addison Airport. From there Gary put me on a jet, still blindfolded, where Gena greeted me and helped me to my seat. Once we took off, Gena said, "OK, now you can take off the blindfold."

"Where are we going?" I asked.

"You'll find out!" she answered.

We landed in Cancun, and Phil Cameron, our personal security person, met us and helped us through the customs process. From there we went to a hotel, where we spent the night.

The following morning, Gena had arranged for a boat to pick us up for what I thought might be a simple, romantic cruise. I should have known better! As we crossed the harbor, I noticed a small plane approaching, an enormous message trailing behind it. As the plane flew closer overhead, I could read the words, "Happy Birthday, Stud-muffin!"

A few moments later another plane appeared in the sky. The plane circled our boat and began dropping roses . . . not a few roses, not rose petals. Thousands of full red roses began dropping from the sky. It looked as though the heavens were raining roses!

We arrived at Isla Muires, a private island where Gena had arranged for me to do something I've always wanted to do —

swim with the dolphins. Afterward we had a quiet, private dinner. It was truly a birthday I will never forget!

I'm not nearly as expressive as Gena or as extravagant in my planning, so for her next birthday I wrote her a song. Anyone who has ever heard me sing knows what a sacrifice that was for me to put my voice on tape and give it to my wife. Gena cried when she heard the song, not because of my poor singing but because of my attempt to express my heartfelt love for her in a fresh, new way.

Certainly not every couple can fly off to Cancun and cause it to rain roses, and not everyone would want to write a song for the person he or she loves. But I'd encourage you to do something creative to make memories with your loved ones. Gena and I try to do special things for each other every day, simply to keep our love fresh and alive, but her exceptional efforts to celebrate my birthday in the year 2000 were more than I could have ever expected.

That same year, I had a great time campaigning for our forty-third President just as I had for the forty-first President twelve years earlier. I first came out strong for

George W. Bush when he campaigned for governor of Texas in 1994 against a formidable foe, incumbent Governor Ann Richards, who was running for a second term. Ms. Richards constantly derided George Bush on television for his conservative views, and her snide, unfair comments annoyed and frustrated me.

I've known George W. since I campaigned for his father in 1988, so when I was asked to join his campaign for governor, I said, "There is nothing I would rather do!" By then our television show, *Walker, Texas Ranger*, was garnering great ratings, and I felt that if my popularity as the star of the show could help George W. Bush's campaign, I was ready.

On the campaign trail, my job was to introduce George W. at rallies. I often started off my speech by telling the crowd how happy I was to be campaigning for George Walker Bush. I'd pause, then say, "*Walker*, . . . I just love that name." The crowd would break out laughing and cheering because they knew that was my character's name on TV.

During one of my speeches introducing George W. as the next governor, I accidentally introduced him as "the next president." I caught myself and said, "No, the next governor, not the next president . . . yet!" That was a real Freudian slip, . . . or maybe I was speaking prophetically and didn't know it!

George W. won the election and became a great governor in Texas. During his time in office, he united our state in many ways and even had the Republicans and the Democrats working together for the benefit of all, no small feat in Texas politics. In fact, when George W. Bush ran for re-election, the late Lt. Governor Bob Bullock, a Democrat, endorsed him, and George W. won by a landslide.

One of the many qualities about the Bush family that I admire is their genuineness. Whether you like them or not, they are what and who they are; there is no pretense about them. They're just real folks.

Former President Bush and his wife, Barbara, invited Gena and me to spend the weekend with them at their home in Kennebunkport, Maine. When we arrived, President Bush was just getting ready to take his speedboat out for a spin. "Come on!" he said. "Come along with me!"

We looked at Barbara, and Gena asked, "Mrs. Bush, are you going?"

Barbara's eyebrows rose, as she said, "Oh, no! You go right ahead."

We climbed into the boat, and the President said, "Gena, you stand up here, next to me." Gena dutifully stepped up to the wheel where President Bush was standing. Meanwhile, I got in the back of the boat along with a Secret Service agent. Three more agents followed us, close behind in a small dinghy.

President Bush had barely pulled away from the dock and into deep waters when he thrust the throttle forward! The speedboat's front end rose in the air, and we roared across the rough waters. Gena was hanging on for dear life! She was so scared; she started laughing hysterically! The President saw Gena laughing and assumed she was having a wonderful time, so he tromped down on the throttle even further! The speedboat was virtually flying across the waves!

I was hanging on the back with the Secret Service agent, who simply shook his head and rolled his eyes, as if to say, "Boys will be boys!"

When any of the Bushes see me today, they greet me with a big bear hug. If you're a friend of anyone in the Bush family, that's what you get. Regardless of your political persuasion, the Bush family is one from whom we can all learn and a family that we can be proud to have representing America. I am honored to call them my friends.

In 1999, I had starred in a CBS Movie of the Week called *The President's Man* that garnered high ratings for the network. I played Jonathan McCord, the President's secret agent who masquerades as a university professor between assignments. Two years later the network wanted another film with me playing the same character.

During the time I was trying to come up with a story idea for the movie, Gena and I had dinner in Dallas with our friends, Charles and Dee Wyly, and Ray and Senator Kay Bailey Hutchison. As I was talking to Senator Hutchison, I asked her what she thought was the greatest threat to America.

"Terrorism," she replied straightforwardly. "Our greatest fear is someone like Osama Bin Laden sneaking a nuclear weapon into our country." Senator Hutchison explained that we had allowed our nation to become vulnerable to such an attack. "During the last eight years under President Clinton's administration, our security measures and enforcement personnel have been drastically reduced," she said. "That concerns me."

It concerned me, too, and I thought that I might be able to shed some light on the problem. After dinner I called my brother, Aaron, and told him to get our scriptwriters to my house first thing in the morning. "I think I have the story line for *President's Man*," I told him.

The story we developed involved a Bin Laden-type terrorist who contacts the President of the United States and threatens to escalate terrorism all over the world unless his holy warriors, incarcerated for their involvement in the 1993 World Trade Center bombing, are released. Of course, the President refuses to give in to his demands.

In our story a nuclear weapon is indeed sneaked into the United States. The President is threatened and told that the nuclear weapon will be detonated if the holy warriors are not released.

That's when I come into the picture, as the President's main man. I sneak into Afghanistan where the lead terrorist is hiding out. I kidnap him and bring him back to the United States for trial. Then the story really begins!

Interestingly, my conversation with Senator Hutchison took place nine months before September 11, 2001. I had finished my last episode of *Walker, Texas Ranger* in

April, then plunged right into working on the sequel to *The President's Man* in May of that year. As we made the film, we thought we were creating a fictitious story; we shuddered at the possibility of something catastrophic happening in our country. We delivered the finished movie print to CBS on September 6, 2001, five days before that horrible day that none of us will ever forget. Ironically, when the print was delivered to CBS, the original title was *The President's Man: Ground Zero*. After 9-11, we changed the title to *The President's Man: A Line in the Sand*.

I pray every day that nothing like 9-11 will ever happen again. But only if we are prepared and our country seeks God in genuine prayer will we prevail.

Robert Urich played the President of the United States in *The President's Man*, and he was the perfect choice. Robert had the strength of character that we were looking for to portray our nation's leader, George W. Bush.

Robert had been fighting synovial cell carcinoma, a very rare cancer that attacks the joints and spreads to the lungs. He'd gone through chemotherapy treatments and had lost all his hair. But Robert was a fighter, and by the time we were ready to begin filming, he had been in remission and was feeling and looking great. He did a fabulous job acting as the president. Then, not long after our show was completed, Robert became ill again. His condition deteriorated quickly. As Robert was lying in his hospital bed fighting to hang on to life, his wife, Heather, whispered, "Let go, Robert. Let go, and come into my heart."

At Heather's words Robert closed his eyes and peacefully passed away.

Robert Urich was only fifty-five years old. I was deeply saddened that Robert had to leave his family and friends at such a young age, just as many others had on September 11, 2001. We never know what a day will bring, but we can know the One who brings the day. Robert's death was a strong reminder to me that a man's life is not built on the years he has lived but on the accomplishments he has achieved and the difference he has made in other people's lives. Only what is done for God will truly last the test of time.

I'm a conservative, politically speaking, and I'm not bashful about saying so. I believe in less government interference in our daily lives and each person taking more responsibility for his or her own actions. I'm convinced that the American people are good people, and if we will stand on our heritage as a nation founded upon Christian values, we can overcome any obstacles that face us.

One day while watching TV, I saw Sean Hannity interviewing David Frum, author of a book on President George W. Bush. Mr. Frum commented that the President doesn't have a good memory and he lacks curiosity, but he has tremendous resolve.

I couldn't vouch for George W.'s memory, but I know his father had an incredible ability to recall details. Once I was at a congressional party with President Bush, and he introduced me to more than forty members of the House of Representatives, by name, without ever having to be prompted. If his son's memory is anything similar, Mr. Frum's opinion is based on misinformation.

The morning after I'd heard Mr. Frum's comment, when Gena and I sat down to read the Bible together, as we do every morning, she turned to Proverbs, chapter 4. Interestingly, the Scripture was about wisdom! The writer of the proverb said that if you want wisdom, you must willfully decide to go after it. It takes resolve, a determination not to abandon the process once you begin, no matter how difficult the road may be. The verse also said that determination is not a once-in-a-lifetime step but a daily process of choosing between right and wrong. That is wisdom! And nothing is more important or valuable than attaining it.

Television interviewers often ask me what I would do if I were president. Most likely I'd follow a path similar to that of George W. Bush, praying and seeking God for wisdom to make right decisions. Many of my own values and personality characteristics are similar to those of George W. Bush. I don't have the greatest memory in the world. I'm impatient if something isn't getting done efficiently. If something doesn't interest me, I don't have the slightest inclination to learn about it. But, if I'm focused on something that I want to accomplish, then I have the tenacity, resolve, determination, and perseverance to keep working until the job is done.

I'm proud, too, of George W. Bush's fearless espousal of his Christian faith. He is not afraid to declare his faith in Christ, not simply some ambiguous "god." Don't think that doesn't cost him political votes. But the man has the courage to tell you what he believes; I like that in a person.

How would I handle difficult issues such

as drug addiction and the related crimes that surround the sale of drugs? I concur with a suggestion made by Bill O'Reilly in his book, *The O'Reilly Factor*. Bill posits his belief that all convicted drug suspects should be given a choice: forced drug rehabilitation in a prison drug facility or a longer sentence to be served within the general prison population. This program was instituted in Alabama, and Bill states that hundreds of pages of statistics on this new program already prove its unusual effectiveness.

Just as Bill O'Reilly believes in forced rehab for convicted drug offenders, I believe there is a better way to punish our juvenile offenders, rather than incarcerating them in a facility that makes bad kids worse. When a juvenile is convicted of a crime, perhaps we ought to consider the benefits of sending him or her on a mission trip, where the young person is obligated to help the starving, the sick, or the disabled, working alongside such benevolent organizations as Larry Jones's Feed the Children or Franklin Graham's Samaritan's Purse. Instead of wasting away behind bars, let kids convicted of crimes work off their time by helping to feed other children. I recognize that organizations such as the ones I mentioned see their mission as part of a spiritual commitment, not merely a deep sense of altruism, but every organization helping to alleviate human suffering needs help, and if juvenile offenders are influenced spiritually while they are helping these modern-day saints, so much the better! I believe that the crime rate would go down, and hurting people would be helped in the process.

Most juvenile offenders are so obsessed with a "the world owes me" attitude that if they were forced to help the less fortunate, they would soon see that life has not really been that hard for them. I believe they would get a whole new positive perspective about their lives. And that would help make our communities better for all of us.

CHAPTER 29

God Has Plans for You!

Gena and I enjoy traveling to various countries around the world. It is always an eye-opener when we encounter the different cultures on the planet. We return home to the United States, thanking God for the many blessings he has bestowed on our country.

During a recent trip to Russia, Gena and I visited a number of countries formerly under the control of the communist rule of the Union of Soviet Socialist Republics. We were invited to visit a country called Kalmykia, a small autonomous country south of Kazakhstan. It is still under a dictatorial form of government, although a much more benign one than that of the previous leaders.

Apparently the people of that nation had seen some of my movies or television shows because they treated us as heroes. The dictator, Kirsan Ilyumzhinov, arranged to have us flown in by private jet. As we deplaned in Kalmykia, we were greeted by a welcoming party of government officials and some of the local population. With cameras rolling, one of the greeters gave us one of their local delicacies to sample, a bowl of something that looked similar to milk. Wanting to be cordial, I took a sip.

I nearly gagged right there on the tarmac! The stuff was awful! I later discovered that the drink was comprised of warm horse milk mixed with butter and salt.

Welcome to Kalmykia!

Our hosts were anxious to show us their culture and how the Mongolians lived during the 1800s, so we viewed their makeshift tents once used for housing, their pig-roasting pits, and various historical displays. It was sort of the Mongolian version of Colonial Williamsburg in Virginia.

At the close of our tour, we went to an archery range where some of the Kalmykia sharpshooters were practicing. One of the local experts brought over a bow and arrow to me, nodding toward the target. I didn't understand the language, but it was plain to see that he wanted me to try my luck at shooting the bow and arrow.

I pulled on the bowstring and immediately realized that this was no toy. It was strung tightly, and it took a lot of strength simply to pull back the bow.

Oh, no! I thought. *This is going to be really interesting or really embarrassing.*

I was about fifty feet away from the target. I pulled back the bow, aimed as best I could, and let the arrow fly. The arrow streaked through the air almost as though it were on a wire, and smack! It struck the bull's-eye, dead center, right in the middle of the target! It was as though an angel had delivered that shot!

I wish I'd been composed enough to act nonchalantly about the perfect shot, but I was as surprised as anyone. My mouth dropped wide open in amazement.

"Carlos! You did it!" Gena crowed behind me. "You hit the bull's-eye!"

"Yeah, I know. I hope they don't ask me to do it again!"

The dictator's mouth was agape, as well. He rushed over to me, clasped my hands with his, and raised our arms together high in the air in front of the target, clearly showing the arrow in the center, while his staff photographers snapped dozens of pictures.

Later the dictator took us on a tour of the town. We noticed as we went around the community that there were large banners bearing the dictator's picture, as well as other leaders including the pope and several presidents.

Gena whispered under her breath, "The next time we come back here, there will probably be a picture of you and the dictator up on one of those walls, with that arrow in the center of that bull's-eye!"

Our many travels have prepared and conditioned us for what I believe will be an important step in the life of my family and me.

After the wrapping of *Walker*, and the birth of our babies, I began to look at my life and say, "OK, what do you really want to do at this stage of your life?" As odd as it may sound to some, when the twins are a little older, we as a family hope to serve God and help other people by doing missionary work.

One night Gena and I were invited to appear on a television talk show along with some friends of ours. A special guest on the program that night was Larry Jones, head of Feed the Children, a worldwide relief organization based in Tulsa, Oklahoma.

We'd never met Larry before, but Gena and I had seen Larry's programs on television for years, often depicting tragic human need and asking people to respond. Far from a fly-by-night swindler bilking the public, playing upon the compassion of viewers, Larry Jones and his organization have been working for more than thirty years in some of the most difficult situations and most impoverished spots in the world, such as Calcutta, Ethiopia, Mogadishu, Bosnia, and others. They've worked with indefatigable effort, under the worst of conditions, alleviating as much pain and sorrow as possible by feeding the hungry.

As I listened to Larry tell story after story of horrendous human suffering in the world, coupled with incredibly simple, doable opportunities to help, I was inspired by his passion and impressed with his sincerity and his humility. Gena and I fell in love with the man's heart. It seemed that he didn't have a selfish bone in his body, that his entire purpose for living was to help others who are hurting. Besides providing food, clothing, and medicine for children in troubled spots around the world, Larry's organization also provided a helping hand for impoverished people in America.

Although I'd never lived in squalor, I could relate to living in poverty, recalling the tough circumstances in which my mom lived and how hard she worked to keep food on the table for my brothers and me. I knew what it felt like to have no hope and how the good folks from the Calvary Baptist Church had helped Mom when nobody else would or could.

After the show I said to Gena, "Now that's the type of work I would like our family to get involved in."

Gena didn't flinch. "I would love our children to be a part of something like that."

We began pursuing short-term missions opportunities, in which we could serve God and other people. We already have a compassion for kids and have been doing all we can through **KICK**START, our own organization, working with kids in the schools. Working with other mission groups will simply be an expansion of what we are already doing.

Gena has become an integral part of my entire life, including my children, my family relationships, adopting my family history as her own. Our relationships with our children are stronger now than they've ever been. We believe that God has good things in store for each of them.

Over the last two decades, I've spoken on a volunteer basis to thousands of under-privileged youngsters. The most common question they ask me is, "Mr. Norris, what is the secret to your success?"

I respond by saying there is no secret. I explain that there are two distinct paths we can follow in life — a positive path or a negative one. On the positive path you don't wait for things to happen; you make them happen by setting goals and working hard to achieve them, no matter how long it takes.

On the negative path you feel like you can never accomplish anything, and that nothing good will ever come your way. If you say to yourself, "I can't do this or that," *can't* becomes the operative word in your mind and results in a self-fulfilling failure. The person who says, "I *can,*" has already started on the path toward success.

You must be positive about everything you do; otherwise it is easy to become affected by negative thinking. Like it or not, we are surrounded by negative attitudes, words, and thoughts. All you need to do is listen to the people around you. There will always be someone who tells you that you can't achieve something you want because you are not big enough or smart enough, or your skin is not the right color, or your religion is the wrong one, or you are not qualified enough, or you are overqualified. People who tell you these things are frequently not successful themselves.

When I decided to get into films, I was told repeatedly that action films were on the decline; no one was interested in me as an actor because everyone considered me an athlete who had no acting experience. Beyond that, I was thirty-six years of age when I made the transition from being a martial arts teacher to being an actor. To some people I was a has-been before I even started!

If I had accepted such judgments, I would never have made that first movie; nor would I have persisted and made other films after the first. I treated the initial rejections as temporary setbacks because I knew that with enough time, determination, and hard work — along with a faith in God and a positive mental attitude — I would succeed.

Few people become successful overnight at any endeavor. Most successful people have learned to stick with whatever it is they wish to achieve and to work step by step until they reach their objective. That has certainly proven true in my life.

It's been interesting to notice how my priorities have changed in recent years. Many of the cravings and desires that once were part of my life are now gone. Certainly part of that is the result of maturity, a strong commitment to my marriage and family, a deepening of my faith, as well as having more time and financial security than I did in past years. I've learned how to be confident without being cocky. More importantly, I've come to a place of contentment in my life. But contentment does not imply complacency.

People often ask me, "How do you stay in such great shape?"

Truth is, I must work at it, just like anyone else. I get up each morning and work out physically; Gena and I take time each day to read the Bible, pray, and exercise spiritually; having short-term and long-term goals is also important to me; and of course, I have two little children to keep me busy! I don't ever see myself retiring; I always want to be active. I've noticed that many people who retire almost immediately begin to atrophy in every aspect of their lives. Before long they get weak and flabby, physically, intellectually, and spiritually. Besides, I don't see anything about retirement in the Bible. It seems to me that God expects us to keep living every day of life to the fullest, believing every morning that "God has plans for you!"

In many ways I believe my best days are still ahead, that everything up to this point is preparatory for something that God wants me to do. I wake up each morning, watching for the opportunities to do something that others say can't be done. I still think young; I feel young, and I never want to lose that attitude.

Gena loves to quip that she expects to celebrate our fiftieth wedding anniversary in Hawaii. "No pressure, honey," she tells me. Of course, that means that I'll have to keep myself mentally, physically, and spiritually sharp for a while. On our fiftieth anniversary, I will be 108 years old!

But I'm planning to be there. Why? Because I believe I can do all things through Christ who strengthens me.

Besides, I like living . . . *Against All Odds!*

About the Authors

Chuck Norris is known as an action-adventure movie and television star, but considers his humanitarian works his greatest accomplishments. Along with participating with the United Way, Make-A-Wish Foundation®, and the Veterans Administration, among others, he counts his most rewarding accomplishment as being the creator of the Kick Drugs Out of America Foundation (**KICK**START) to help at-risk kids raise their self-esteem and instill discipline and respect. He, Gena, and their children live in Dallas, Texas.

Ken Abraham is a *New York Times* bestselling author known around the world for his collaborations with high-profile public figures. His recent books include *Let's Roll!*, with Lisa Beamer, widow of United Flight 93 hero Todd Beamer as well as the fiction series *The Prodigal Project*. He also cowrote *Payne Stewart: The Authorized Biography* with Tracey Stewart, widow of Payne Stewart.